Inside the
Bungalow

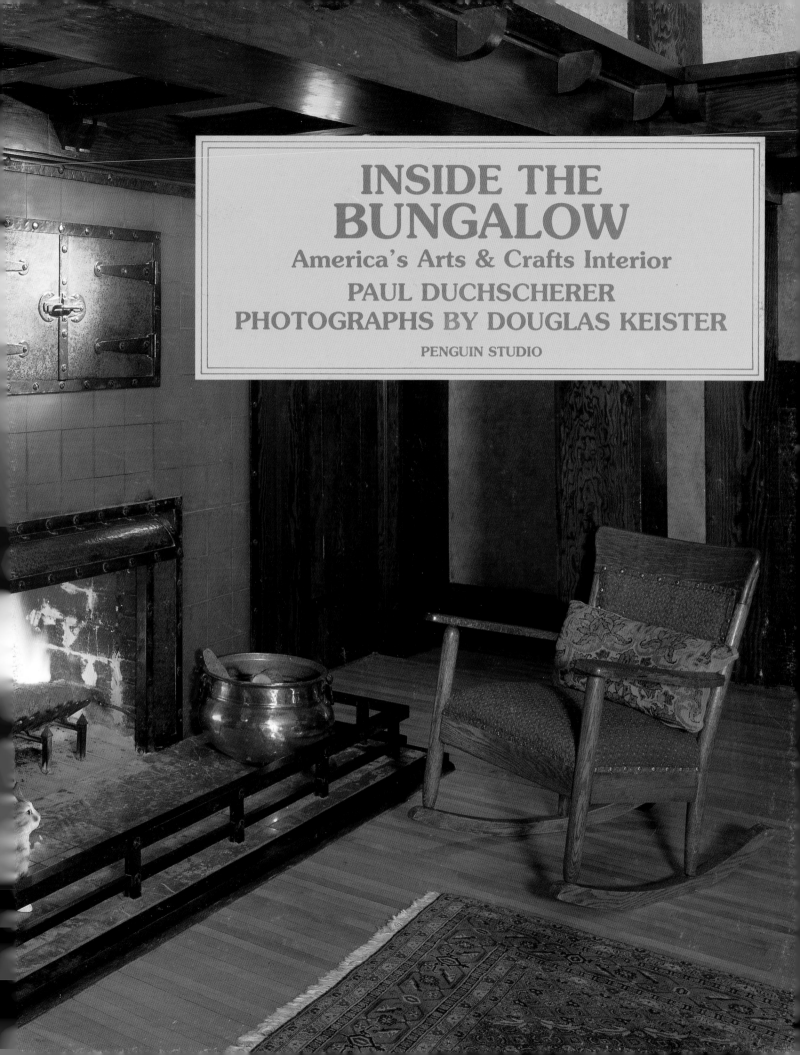

INSIDE THE BUNGALOW
America's Arts & Crafts Interior

PAUL DUCHSCHERER
PHOTOGRAPHS BY DOUGLAS KEISTER

PENGUIN STUDIO

(Overleaf) Fireplace in Spokane, Washington. This fireplace forms a harmonious ensemble with its surrounding architecture. In a classic expression of the Arts and Crafts aesthetic, each element contributes to, but does not overwhelm, the overall design. Records show that the house was built in 1907 on a wooded hillside in the South Hill district of Spokane, a neighborhood rich in early twentieth-century architecture. Just out of view to the right a small peaked ceiling creates an entry vestibule open to the living room (fig. 23). Adjacent to it is this fireplace alcove at one end of the room. Leading to a pair of bedrooms, the two doors flanking the fireplace have simple, vertical planks of fir, and are fitted with original art-glass panels and hand-wrought hardware. Faint outlines, still visible on the woodwork, indicate that a pair of square columns once supported the dropped beam that spans this alcove. Also missing is a pair of built-in benches that once framed the fireplace, which shows that it was conceived as a true inglenook. The current owners are still renovating the house and plan to restore the missing elements. As the focal point of the living room, the fireplace dominates the space with the deep terra cotta of its original matte-glazed tiles. Framed by a riveted, hand-hammered iron surround, the tile facing is crisply defined. Centered above the fireplace opening, a pair of hand-hammered copper doors is framed by boldly riveted iron and displays matching strap hinges and a distinctive latch. The craftsmanship of these doors belies their rather mundane purpose—to conceal the damper mechanism. More superb metalwork of the period is seen in the original copper lantern sconces that hang from hand-hammered backplates on either side of the fireplace. (For other views of this house see figs. 23, 46.)

PENGUIN STUDIO
Published by the Penguin Group
Penguin Putnam Inc., 375 Hudson Street,
New York, New York, 10014, U.S.A.

Penguin Books Ltd, 27 Wrights Lane,
London W8 5TZ, England

Penguin Books Australia Ltd, Ringwood,
Victoria, Australia

Penguin Books Canada Ltd, 10 Alcorn Avenue, Suite 300,
Toronto, Ontario, Canada M4 V3 B2

Penguin Books (N.Z.) Ltd, 182-90 Wairau Road,
Auckland 10, New Zealand

Penguin Books Ltd, Registered Offices:
Harmondsworth, Middlesex, England

First published by Penguin Studio, a member of Penguin Putnam Inc.

First printing, November 1997
10 9 8 7 6 5 4

Copyright © Paul Duchscherer and Douglas Keister 1997
All rights reserved.

Library of Congress Catalog Card Number: 97-66505

Book designed by Marilyn Rey
Printed and bound by Dai Nippon Printing Co., Hong Kong, Ltd.

ISBN: 0-670-87373-X

This book is dedicated to the proud homeowners
who opened their homes to us, and to all
others who will find inspiration here
for their own hearths and homes.

ACKNOWLEDGMENTS

We wish to extend our deepest gratitude, appreciation, and thanks to the following homeowners, whose generosity in sharing their personal environments has made this book possible: Louise and David Adams, Joyce Albers and Jerry Mendelsohn, Arlene Baxter / *Arts & Crafts Homes*, Terry Bible, Carol and David Blomgren, Judith Bond, Eleanor and Chris Burian-Mohr, Charlene Casey, Patricia and Robert Coe, Suzanne and Frank Cooper, Karen and Don Covington, Cathie and Bill Daniels, Louis F. D'Elia, Lori and Michael Delman, Sammie and Robert Dunn, Elisabeth Ekman, Stephen J. Franks, Lauren Gabor and Scott D. Goldstein, Claudia Geletka and Rob Winovich, Robin and Sydney Galer, Vicki D. Granowitz and William R. Lees, Lauren Rickey Greene and David Greene, Austene Hall and Robert Archibald, Aaron Hammons, Ingrid Helton and Erik Hanson, Joan and Rex Hollowell, Glen Jarvis / Jarvis Architects, Lani and Larry Johnson / The Johnson Partnership, William Joliff, Beth and Chris Kelleher, Janene and Michael Khanchalian, Lina and Wayne Knowles, Lawrence Kreisman and Wayne Dodge, Craig A. Kuhns, Elinor and Glenn Kuhns, Lynne McDaniel, Janet Mark and Terry Geiser, Vykki Mende Gray and David Swarens, Mr. and Mrs. Wally Haas, Janie and William Jones, Robert Kneisel, Bonnie and Brian Scot Krueger, Paul Lanouette and James Stefanucci, Marilee Marshall and Bruce Wright, Claudia and James D. McCord, Valerie and Kelly McKenzie, Ricardo Mendoza, Monty Montgomery, David Mostardi, Anthony Newcomb, Valorie Olsen, Kathy O'Neal, Melissa Patton, Marsha Perloff, Jerry Peters, Holly and Kurt Peterson, Catherine and Louis Phelps, Pat and Rod Poole, Bonnie Poppe, Betsy Priddy and Jimmy Onstott, John H. Phillips, Marilyn Raack and Jim Bixler, Julie Reiz and Ken Miedema, Judith Rees, Marjorie Rohmer, Chuck Roché and Joseph Ryan, Taly Rutenberg and Joel ben Izzy, Maxine and James Risley, Marnie Ross, Randy Sappenfield, Joan Seear, Jane Shabaker, Don Shelman / Avenue Antiques, Charlotte White Simpson, Frances and Gary Spradlin, Tracy Stone and Joseph DeSousa, Juliet and Charles Sykes, Lynda and Dan Tortarolo / Anjelica's Mansion Bed & Breakfast of Spokane, Pat and Peter Van Valkenburgh, Vreni and Jerry Watt, Don Weggeman and Odell Childress, Zvia and Robert Weinstein / Craftsman Style, Michael Wheelden, Helen Witter and Ahmad Taie, Kelly and Phillip Woods, Larry Word and Don Bean, Martha Works and Paul Hribernick, Virginia Worthington.

The number of people who helped us with this book is remarkable, and we wish it were possible to acknowledge each one here. Their help took many forms, and included everything from shared resources and location referrals to simple moral support. Regardless of their specific contributions, we offer each one our heartfelt thanks for every kindness and courtesy extended to us along the way: Alameda Victorian Preservation Society, Albany (Oregon) Visitors Association / Julie Jackson, *American Bungalow* Magazine / John Brinkman and George Murray, American Decorative Arts Forum / Don Miller, Arroyo Style / Laurie King / David Heller, Artistic License of San Francisco, Michael Ashford, Dianne Ayres and Timothy Hansen / Arts & Crafts Period Textiles, Bennye and Richard Bail, John Benriter, David Berman, Dr. and Mrs. Duane Bietz, Edward R. Bosley / Gamble House staff, Agnes Bourne, Helen Boutell, Elise Brewster and Paul Smith / Kallos, Bradbury & Bradbury Art Wallpapers / Bruce Bradbury, Scott Cazet, Jill Harris, Jan McHargue, Therese Tierney, Ken Sarna and the Bradbury production staff, Peter Bridgman, Paula and Brewster Brock, Jane and Gus Browne, Anthony Bruce / Berkeley Architectural Heritage Association, Chris Buckley, Madeleine Burke, Murray Burns, John Burrows / J.R. Burrows & Company, Ann and Andre Chaves, Bruce Chevillat, Kay and Robert Cheatham, Cheney Cowles Museum / Glen Mason and Marsha Rooney, Phil Chun / Craftsman Antiques, Dale Clark, Johanna and Tom Clark, Robert Judson Clark, Brian Coleman and Howard Cohen, Craftsman Style / Robert and Zvia Weinstein and Bridgid Faith, Riley Doty / Doty Tile, Dovetale Publishers / William J. O'Donnell, Becky Bernie and Sherrie Somers; Leon F. Drozd, Jr., Mr. and Mrs. James P. Duchscherer, Kenneth J. Duchscherer, Hank Dunlop / Victorian Preservation Center of Oakland / Cohen-Bray House, Robin and Robert Ebinger, Echo Park Historical Society, Lucinda Eddy / Marston House / Museums of San Diego History, Betty and Sam Eisenstein, Anita Feder-Chernila and David Miller, George Fleerlage, Linda Forshay, Helen Foster / Helen Foster Stencils, Nancy and Jim Fullmer, Arrol Gellner, Ora Gosey, Dan Gregory / *Sunset Magazine*, Jackie and Robert Gustafson, Julie Hardgrove and Cliff Cline, Jodi Larusson Harris, David B. Hellman, Richard Hilkert, Historic Preservation League of Oregon / Lisa Burcham, William J. Hawkins III, Timothy Holton / Holton Furniture and Frame, Constance Hornig and Ted Humphreville, Dawn and Steven Jacobsen, Tim Jackson, Lee Jester / The Craftsman Home, Karen Kees, Katherine Keister, Deborah and Peter Keresztury, Peggy King and Damian Martin, Laurie and Matt Knowles, Henry Kunowski, John Kurtz, Laguna/Bif Brayman and Michael Lindsay, Cornelia and Kerry Lange, Avner Lapovsky, Jeanne and Mark Lazzarini, Jack Leutza, Jeremy Levine, Kris Maas, Ronald MacArthur, Caro Macpherson, Mimi Manning, James M. Marrin, Randell L. Makinson, Stephanie McCoy, Roy McMakin, George A. McMath, Carol Mead, Mary Lou and Ron Miller, Brenda Beers Mock, Elizabeth A. Moore and Oger Owner, Gretchen Muller, Davis Musser, Jackie and Tom Newcomb, New England Guild of Artisans, Robert J. Noble / Lifetime Gallery, Oakland Architectural Heritage Association, Judy O'Boyle and Tim Johnston, Pasadena Heritage / Marguerite Duncan Abrams, Suzanne Peery, David Pennington, Linda Pettavino, Pinson and Ware / Ed Pinson and Debra Ware, Michelle Plochere and David Dalzell, Lily Pond, *Old House Interiors* / Patricia Poore, *Old House Journal* / Gordon Bock, Clare Porter, Jane Powell, Roger Pritchard, Rejuvenation Lamp and Fixture Company / Jim Kelly, Bill Welch, and staff, David Raposa and Ed Trosper / City Living Realty, Dave and Marina Rogers, Charles Rupert Designs / Margaret Graham-Bell and Stuart Stark, Nancy Saltair and Peter Garrison, Ann Sansberry, Save Our Heritage Organization / Bill Lawrence, Ted Schneider, Keith Schroeder / Castro Photo, Juliana Scuam and Mark Mansfield, Seattle Art Museum / Julie Emerson, Kris Sheehan, Sigma Phi Society / Thorsen House, Signature Homes / John Apelt, Rob Sissman, Bruce Smith and Yoshiko Yamamoto / The Arts & Crafts Press / *The Tabby*, Marcia Smith, William Steelman / RAI/EGI Exhibitions, Inc., Nancy Stillger / Ainsley House, *Style 1900* / David Rago and Kristen Hodgson, Pat Suzuki, Laurie Taylor / Ivy Hill Interiors, Marty and Ron Thomas / *Bungalows*, Kitty Turgeon and Robert Rust / Foundation for the Study of the Arts & Crafts Movement at Roycroft, Victorian Preservation Association of San Jose, Elder Vides / Painting Concepts, Mary Ann and Steve Voorhees / Voorhees Craftsman, Marti Wachtel, Ann Wallace / Ann Wallace & Friends, Mary Ward, Martin Eli Weil, West Adams Historical Association, Brian Westmoreland, United Crafts / Sarah Wildasin, Roger L. Conant Williams, Peggy Wilson and John Stone, Dr. Robert Winter, Diana Woodbridge, Sandy Wynn and Steven Duchscherer, George Zaffle, John Zanakis and Arthur van der Beek / House of Orange, Tracy Zeluff and John Grant, Debey Zito and Terry Schmitt.

Endless thanks for the supreme efforts of our editor and guiding light, Cyril I. Nelson, whose help and support throughout has been continuous and enthusiastic. With a special salute, our final thanks are given to three remarkable people who helped us in extraordinary ways, too numerous to mention here: Sandy Schweitzer, John Freed, and Don Merrill. Far beyond the call of duty, each gave us phenomenal support, encouragement, and assistance that is appreciated more than they already know.

CONTENTS

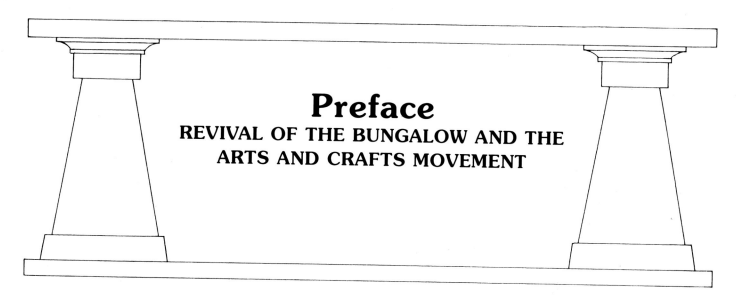

Preface
REVIVAL OF THE BUNGALOW AND THE ARTS AND CRAFTS MOVEMENT

Fortunately for old houses, the historic preservation movement in America has never been stronger. Its horizons of concern now stretch from the pre-Colonial era well into the twentieth century. But can houses of more recent vintage also be considered historic? Some developers maintain that many small, less-imposing homes of the modern period (i.e. bungalows) are not worthy of preservation. In cities with high property values a "tear-down" approach often prevails. A small home on a large lot can be demolished in the name of land-use efficiency in order to rebuild on a larger scale. Many of our communities place a high priority on creating short-term jobs generated by new construction. Preserving and restoring examples of our architectural heritage usually require fewer but more highly skilled craftspeople, and doing so isn't often a priority. This dilemma is likely to continue, and the preservation movement will certainly have its share of future battles. One of its best weapons is tirelessly to educate the public to understand the cultural importance of historic preservation. Once gone, an old building is not a renewable resource.

Over the past several years, the surge of public interest in the bungalow has established it as America's newest "historic house." Because history has a way of repeating itself, the bungalow could once again become America's

favorite house, for during the first three decades of this century, that is exactly what it was. Then, after peaking in popularity during the Twenties, shifting public tastes and the economics of the Great Depression led to its subsequent decline. Why is the bungalow making such a strong comeback? Nostalgia for the past, particularly at the end of this century, is probably a contributing factor. Another major reason is that there are still quite a number of them around. Cities across America have whole neighborhoods filled with bungalows, many languishing in obscurity in long-unfashionable areas. Many homes in these areas have been rental properties for years, often with absentee landlords who have not kept up routine maintenance, so many bungalows have been subjected to long-term abuse rather than to loving care. Many have been lost altogether to fire or to misguided redevelopment.

Having gathered momentum through increased public interest and participation over the past two decades, the flourishing restoration movement embraces all kinds of old houses. Because bungalows are generally more affordable to purchase and restore than some older houses, some of America's bungalow neighborhoods are veritable hotbeds of restoration fever. A first-class example of this is the neighborhood in Pasadena, California, officially designated in 1989 as the "Bungalow Heaven Landmark

(Opposite) Entering a living room in Marin County, California. With the characteristic informality of a bungalow, the front door opens right into the living area, where this single room serves both as a living room and dining room. Recently renovated, it is a showcase for the artistry and skill of many craftspeople from both the past and present. A fine collection of decorative arts of the period is the focus of the owner's passion for the Arts and Crafts style. The quarter-sawn oak front door, a classic bungalow design, was salvaged from another location and fitted with handsome art-glass panels of the period. Creating a warm welcome is the fireplace, recently fitted with an original oak mantel that has simple lines in the Craftsman taste. Its two-tiered design incorporates sturdy shelves, a beveled mirror, and square columns set on point. The fireplace surround and hearth are faced with handmade blue-green tiles, and the andirons, freestanding firescreen, and tool set were handcrafted in period designs. The owner has a particular interest in period lighting, and every room has fine examples. The ceiling fixture, with its distinctive triangulated backplate and four decorated glass shades, and the elegant art-glass floorlamp were both made by Handel. Early California landscape paintings appear throughout the house. Because there were no coffee tables manufactured in the Craftsman era, a conveniently scaled bench of the period has been placed in front of a large oak settle. The frieze area of the walls awaits the application of a handpainted, stylized landscape design, which will encircle the entire room. (For other views of this house see figs. 69, 87, 110, 120, 121.)

1. Design for a bungalow. Although they were actually built in a surprising variety of styles and shapes, here is a classic design for a bungalow. In the mid-Teens, the heyday of the bungalow, this particular design appeared in a catalog of the Eberson Paint Company, which had manufacturing locations in St. Louis and Baltimore. Probably to increase its appeal, the designer chose to combine two of the most popular new-house styles of the day, Craftsman and Colonial Revival. The use of river rock on the piers of the porch columns, chimney, and foundation was a favorite device of the Craftsman style. Another Craftsman touch is the use of exposed rafter tails that project from beneath the deep eaves, which shows how a structural element can also become a decorative feature. The Colonial Revival style, which outlasted the Craftsman, is seen in the pyramidal hipped roof, the round columns, the narrow clapboard siding, the turned balusters of the porch railing, and the detailing of the front door and multipaned windows.

District." Once ailing, it is now often cited as a model for similar neighborhoods on the rebound across every part of this country. Reflecting renewed public interest, demand, owner energy, and pride of place, long-flat housing prices are also on the rise in many such areas. While every bungalow today is probably not the bargain it once was, the majority of them still represent good value, especially when compared to comparably priced, newly constructed homes.

More than most historic-building types, the bungalow tells some rather illuminating stories about American character, ingenuity, and social history, such as the account of its almost explosive development. Fueled by low cost, convenience, and novelty, house plans or entirely prefabricated houses were made easily available by mail order. Waves of "bungalow mania" swept various parts of the country, particularly in California and Florida, and thus helped to create real-estate "booms." Inspired by these successes, other promoters and developers nationwide were quick to present the relative ease of bungalow ownership to an eager public, and their success in accommodating first-time buyers is legendary. It took the Great Depression to put a major crimp in the bungalow business.

The bungalow originated in the Bengal region of India. Evolving from an indigenous native hut called a *bangala*, this word gradually became anglicized as *bungalow*. The overall form of the *bangala* was defined by a high thatched roof with overhanging eaves, which shaded its single-story mud walls from the sun. Long before bungalows appeared in America, they were adapted by the British as practical housing for colonials stationed in distant outposts of the empire. Eventually, the bungalow became associated with leisure architecture. In England, the compact and no-frills housing units popular in seaside resort towns came to be called bungalows. The term also came to be used for small houses in suburban real-estate developments of industrialized English cities.

Becoming popular in America, most likely by way of English books and periodicals, the term *bungalow* was used as early as 1880 to describe a summer house in an American architectural journal. Here, as in England, a fairly diverse range of dwellings came to be referred to as bungalows for they included vacation lodgings as well as comfortable year-round homes for the middle classes. From the street, budding bungalow-watchers will learn that there are plenty of quirky variations to be seen in

these houses. They will discover, with experience, that the outside doesn't always reveal the inner charm of a house, or other mysteries such as its floorplan. Once inside, there may well be more rewards than what was implied by the exterior.

In America, around the turn of the century, bungalows became increasingly associated with the Arts and Crafts Movement, another British import. It was a spirited reform movement, centered on the idea of preserving age-old traditions of handcraftsmanship in the wake of the Industrial Revolution. A diminishing supply of well-designed and handmade goods, especially home furnishings, steered the Movement's proponents in mostly artistic directions. In vogue with the progressively minded near

2. View through the front door of the Oscar Maurer house in Berkeley, California. For many, the special appeal of the bungalow lies in the fact that bungalows inspire feelings of warmth and security, as can readily be seen when one peers through the iron grille of a small window in the front door of this turn-of-the-century house. The simple offering of good cheer by a warm fireside is beguiling, and the spell is cast. We are drawn closer by the glow of natural wood and absorbed by the surrounding play of light, color, and texture. (For other views of this house see figs. 26, 119.)

the turn of the century was a concern for the well-being of the factory worker, which also peripherally linked the Movement to Socialist causes.

American public awareness of the Arts and Crafts Movement, and encouragement to participate in it actively, was well provided by *The Craftsman* magazine, which was published by Gustav Stickley between 1901 and 1916. Initially inspired by the Movement in England and especially by the work of its influential leader William Morris (1834–1896), this celebrated journal became a lively forum for presenting new ideas on how to live the "Craftsman" life. It often included glowing praise and promotion for the bungalow. Other popular periodicals and design-advice books followed Stickley's lead, and soon the bungalow was officially regarded as an ideal vehicle for artistic self-expression. Indeed, bungalows managed to become popularly perceived as dwellings for the socially enlightened. Embodying ideas of the Movement's leaders, the bungalow's unassuming demeanor and informal character was particularly conducive to enrichment by the use of simple, natural materials and restful color palettes in harmony with its natural setting. Stickley and others soon

saw opportunity in this, and made a good business of publicizing the cozy charms of bungalow life. They also made a good business of supplying the public with everything from house plans to the appropriate furnishings.

Not only attractive to devotees of the Arts and Crafts Movement, the prospect of a home that combined the solid values of practicality, simplicity, and individuality in an affordable and fashionable package was irresistible. Forming the biggest potential bungalow market were the working and middle classes, for whom the American dream of owning one's own home and garden had a powerful appeal. Serving to forge its romanticized image elsewhere was the early and well-publicized popularity of this housing form in trend-setting California.

Quickly gathering a devoted national following, the "cult of the bungalow" generated from owners as well as promoters spirited testimonials such as the slightly outlandish claim that living in one would foster a healthier, happier home and family life. The importance of fresh air to good health was widely associated with these many-windowed houses and their typically open, flowing interior spaces. The popularity of the indoor/outdoor sleeping porch best

3. Design for a living room. Here is a fine rendering of the welcoming informality that in its heyday made the bungalow America's favorite house. The characteristic flow between indoor and outdoor spaces is demonstrated by the view through the French doors to the porch with its built-in bench. The beamed ceiling of natural wood is linked by woodwork to built-in bookcases that are situated next to a built-in bench. Blending well with the wood tones, the walls are painted the soft peach color found in the curtain fabric, and the same fabric is used for the portière in the doorway. Opposite the French doors, the overstuffed rocker at left hints that there may be a fireplace next to it. While this appealing image might also sell houses, it was used here to help sell the rug. The illustration appeared in a catalog published by the Olson Rug Company in the later Twenties. Their most popular designs included machine-made Oriental-style, bordered, and solid-color area rugs. At that time, they had been in business for over fifty years, and their line was manufactured from recycled, so-called "old material," which included worn-out rugs and cast-off woolen clothing, which they actively solicited from their customers. Prices listed in the catalog ranged from a low of $2.55 for a 27" x 42" rug, which required submission of three pounds of "old material," to a high of $50.60 for a 12' x 15' rug, for which seventy-three pounds were needed.

4. Design for a living room with an inglenook and a den. This illustration from the 1916–1917 catalog of James Davis Artistic Paperhangings of Chicago showcases the effects that could be achieved with its products, which were designed to replicate hand-painted finishes and stenciling. As the Twenties neared, public interest toward historical-revival styles was increasing. This illustration, a fine example of the popular taste of that moment, shows how the Craftsman style, just past its peak, could be effectively combined with the Colonial Revival style, which was becoming more important. To be seen mostly in the furniture illustrated here, the Colonial Revival style is found in the oval-back armchair in front of the bookcase, in the armchair at the desk at the left, and in the turned legs of the table and another armchair in the den. It is also seen in the oval divisions in the glass doors of the bookcase, the doorway frames, and the paneled back of the built-in bench. However, Craftsman style is still much in evidence in the living room's beamed ceiling, the cozy inglenook, and the built-in bookcase and drawer unit. Particularly characteristic of the Craftsman style is the subdued color palette used for the walls, curtains, upholstery, and area rugs. Note how the dark green tile of the fireplace surround is used on the floor of the inglenook. Harmonizing well with the tones of natural wood, the warm, earthy colors are similar to those seen in Arts and Crafts textiles and pottery. Simulating an effect that was sometimes referred to as a "Tiffany finish," the blended colors of the wallcoverings replicate handpainted wall finishes. The wallpaper frieze in the living room suggests a series of cutout openings looking out to a landscape and skillfully imitates handpainting and stenciling. In the den is a wallpaper pendant frieze with stylized floral forms set into a bold geometric framework.

expressed this minor obsession. Most bungalow floorplans encouraged a fusion of indoor and outdoor living on a regular basis. Their interior compactness was liberated by generous porches, extra outside doors, and a preponderance of built-in furniture. Although its promotional hype seemed to promise almost too much for a mere house to fulfill, the bungalow delivered on most claims rather well.

The bungalow also received occasional criticism. Faddishness was increasingly linked to the bungalow craze, for once the bungalow was eagerly adopted by so many working people who had little or no awareness of the Arts and Crafts Movement, much of its high-minded and idealistic image evaporated. Its once-innovative features began to seem dated to those who had grown up with them, and by 1930 the younger generation was more likely to want a "cottage" as their first home. Then as now, fashion wields great power in America.

Emerging triumphant today from a somewhat dubious interim legacy (it inspired countless tracts of post-World War II "ranch" houses), the bungalow has come full circle. It is once again savored for its own sake, a piece of our past that still works. The current revival of interest in bungalows parallels the strong revival of the Arts and Crafts Movement. The public's awareness of this movement has actually been expanding steadily over the past two decades, and is presently reflected in the rising values of its highly collectible decorative arts. Just a gradual process until quite recently, examples of the Arts and Crafts design influence are cropping up everywhere, from the set designs of movies and television shows to trendy home-furnishings catalogs. With the recognition of his name further enhanced by publicity and a 1996 exhibition marking the centenary year of his death, the reproduced wallpaper and textile designs of William Morris are the most widely recognized evidence of the style. The celebrated work of America's Arts and Crafts Movement leaders, including Gustav Stickley and the Roycrofters, has taken much of the spotlight in recent years. Already showcased in many prestigious museum collections, traveling exhibitions have displayed their work to expanded audiences. Also emerging as coveted collectibles are the expressive, handcrafted designs of many other manufacturers and craftspeople of the period, including splendid examples of furniture, ceramics, metalwork, glass, and textiles. Defining the "working revival" of the Movement are many successful new artisans and craftspeople across the country, whose inspired work skillfully adapts or reproduces Arts and Crafts designs.

It was only a matter of time before the bungalow itself would be rescued from its long-term obscurity and begin again to be actively recognized for its connections to the Arts and Crafts Movement by an admiring audience. What could provide a better setting for original or recreated treasures from the period than a bungalow? The revival of interest in bungalows has created increased demand for more information and design advice, hence the recent appearance of related books and periodicals.

Since its publication in December 1995, many readers of *The Bungalow: America's Arts & Crafts Home* have requested additional information on and illustrations of bungalow interiors. Period-style kitchens and bathrooms were especially asked for, together with period fireplaces, wall finishes, lighting, and millwork details. It was due to such specific and enthusiastic feedback that this second volume has been assembled.

Some of the same houses originally featured in *The Bungalow* were revisited for additional interior photographs. To facilitate and encourage the reader's interaction between both books, such cross-connections are duly noted when they occur.

In planning this book, it was decided that multiple examples of specific room types or details would be best shown in separate chapters. In anticipation that some readers will wish to view collectively material taken from the same house, such examples are accordingly cross-referenced. Photographs of the work of Charles Sumner Greene and Henry Mather Greene were taken at both the Thorsen and Gamble houses and are shown in their own chapter. The "Before and After" rooms were also combined, regardless of room type, to achieve the greatest visual impact.

Although it is a sequel to *The Bungalow*, this book was conceived to stand on its own. However, should a reader of this book be unacquainted with *The Bungalow*, its features include an expanded historic overview of the Arts and Crafts Movement, a wide range of bungalow exterior styles, and a selection of both old and new Arts and Crafts interiors. It is recommended as a source of additional background material.

The many rooms and their details that follow illustrate the thought and careful planning inherent in bungalow interiors. The pioneering advances in technology incorporated in the kitchens and bathrooms contrast strikingly with the quaintness and coziness found in most of the interiors that have beguiled so many. The bungalow mirrors a paradox of our modern age: we crave efficiency and convenience, but also want comfort and reassurance. Despite a long journey through the twentieth century to its current ascendancy, one of the most endearing and enduring attributes of the bungalow remains its appealingly human scale. These were houses designed for people, and they still come close to a perfect fit.

PAUL DUCHSCHERER

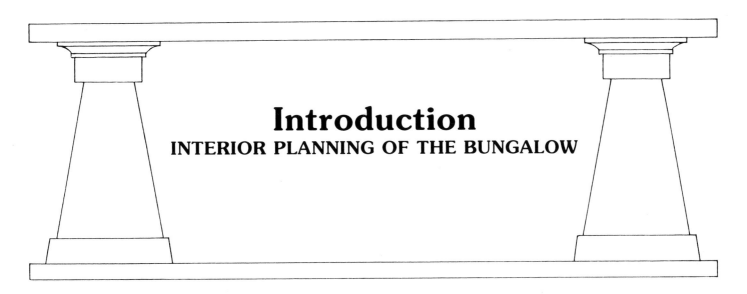

Introduction
INTERIOR PLANNING OF THE BUNGALOW

A distinctive planning approach characterizes most bungalow interiors and, accordingly, sets them apart. While not every design concept associated with the bungalow was new, their combined impact produced a variety of floor plans that was considered modern and innovative. The guiding design priorities of convenience, practicality, and flexibility in most of these plans continue to allow these homes to function well today. Also enhancing the best of bungalow designs were the intertwined goals of simplicity and economy. Driven by the constraints of their typical compactness, a preponderance of care was given to planning the smallest interior details that often recall the design approach used for a ship's cabin. A valid lesson many bungalow plans can teach today's designers is that practical, comfortable living space doesn't necessarily have to be large to function well.

Who was responsible for designing the multitudes of bungalows across America? The answer, in most cases, is that we don't really know. While some custom-built, one-of-a-kind bungalows can be documented to specific architects, they are not common. Sometimes, with homes that are likely to have been architect-designed, the name of the designer has somehow become lost. As a result of the revival of interest in the Arts and Crafts Movement, homes that can be firmly documented to have been built to plans published or designed by Gustav Stickley are enjoying a renewed cachet. However, the vast majority of bungalows were constructed to plans selected and obtained from popular house catalogs, generally known as plan books, which typically didn't credit the name of their architects or designers, some of whom were anonymous and probably underpaid draftsmen. In such a competitive business, it was not uncommon for design plagiarism to blur further the exact origins of a particularly popular house plan. Whether or not the work featured was uniformly theirs,

sometimes the owner of a plan-book company personally received the design credit. Much remains to be discovered about the design origins of our bungalows.

The convenience and success of plan books ensured their rapid proliferation. For a complete set of plans, a prospective homeowner was likely to spend a mere ten to twenty-five dollars, and any plan could be easily modified to meet specific needs, or adapted to accommodate regional differences in building materials, or even site orientation. Once a building lot was secured, it was usual for the owner to provide his plan of choice to a local contractor hired to build the house. Many bungalow-tract developments were built from a range of pre-selected plan-book houses, offered in tempting package deals, complete with the house lots, to any interested and easily qualified buyer.

Modern building techniques played a part in energizing the bungalow boom by allowing homes to be constructed in short time periods. Possible in a lumber-rich nation, wood-frame construction was the most popular type in America. Actually developed to address burgeoning new housing needs that arose in the nineteenth century, a building technique known as "balloon framing," a reference to the speed in which it allowed a house to "go up," had already greatly streamlined the wooden house-building process. Through the pre-assembly of modular sections of structural wood framing at the building site, walls could be quickly constructed, hoisted, and secured into place on their foundation. Homes built in this way were not only raised quickly, but were of remarkably strong and enduring construction, as evidenced by the nearly countless bungalows and many other older wooden houses nationwide.

Another major driving force in the proliferation of bungalows on the American landscape was the advent of the "ready-cut" (or pre-milled) house, which was also marketed through plan books. A buyer could actually order by

BUNGALOW MAGAZINE

OCTOBER 1915
25 CENTS

Supplement Bungalow
Complete Working Drawings,
Specifications and Bill of Material in this Issue

mail a complete package of carefully labeled house parts to be delivered to the building site for assembly. This package could include not only the structural elements of the house, but all the built-in furniture, fixtures, and finished millwork as well. Many different finishing options were available, with handier homeowners able to save considerable sums by doing much or all of the work themselves, from wiring, plumbing, and roofing to interior-finish plastering and woodwork. The ultimate in construction convenience, even impressive two-story houses were as readily available in ready-cut form as the ubiquitous bungalow. This burgeoning business was dominated by retail giant Sears, Roebuck and Company, which was offering ready-cut homes as early as 1909. Montgomery Ward soon followed. Among the better known of the other companies that sold such homes nationally was Alladin Homes of Bay City, Michigan, whose designs also reflected the same popular taste seen in other plan books. The Great Depression years were unkind to this industry, and many companies folded in the wake of rampant foreclosures on homes and land they had eagerly financed. While ready-cut houses survive in great numbers, many current owners are as yet unaware of their true origins. Assisted by a number of reprinted plan books of ready-cut houses such as those by

5. *(Opposite)* Cover of *Bungalow Magazine,* October 1915. This monthly periodical was published in Seattle between 1912 and 1918 by an enterprising businessman named Henry L. Wilson, who had started it in Los Angeles between 1909 and 1910. It was in Southern California, through his efforts at self-promotion, that Wilson gained some renown as the "Bungalow Man." Trained as an architect, he had a successful plan-book business (fig. 8), and he also sold drawings for making bungalow built-ins. When this house was depicted on the cover of *Bungalow Magazine,* it had recently been built with many similar houses in a Seattle neighborhood near Cowan Park. Now well-concealed behind overgrown shrubbery, this bungalow still survives. The magazine's cover story about it included several interior photographs. The "supplement bungalow" cited on the cover was a bonus that included two large folded sheets of complete architectural working drawings, the building specifications, and a "bill of material." Designed as a promotional gift, the insert was intended to entice people to consider the many other house designs that could be purchased from Henry Wilson's plan books. Designed in the Craftsman style, this bungalow features an unusually extensive use of clinker brick, which completely covers its foundation level and continues up onto its porch piers and tall chimney. The mass of brick is relieved by the "eyebrow" slits at the level of the porch floor, which serve as drains. Clinker brick was used extensively for Craftsman-style houses, both inside and out, being prized for its irregular character and varied coloring. Projecting at the right is a second porch that is entered from the dining room.

Sears, there is growing interest nationwide in rediscovering the particular pedigree of such houses.

How a bungalow was positioned within the confines of its site was an important consideration. Usually set back from the street, allowance for a front garden area and, perhaps, something more than just a straight path to the front door enhanced their sense of intimacy. At the same time, views from the porch and the interior gave occupants a sense of openness that belied any smallness of scale. The bungalow garden, also the subject of much attention in design books and periodicals such as *The Craftsman* magazine, was considered of integral importance to the house. Architectural elements such as vine-covered pergolas (fig. 7) and arbors often served to link a house physically with its surrounding vegetation, and also created pleasant enclaves of open-air seating close to the house. Associated with the healthful and artistic qualities of bungalow life was the concept of an outdoor room, where the rusticity of nature could be combined with such civilized provisions as comfortable seating and shade.

Bungalow-interior plans were deliberately designed to feel larger than their typically modest scale suggests. Beginning outside, this effect is usually achieved with a generous covered porch (fig. 5), forming a pleasant and usable transitional area from the street and front garden to the interior beyond. Widely promoted by bungalow planners like Gustav Stickley as the "outdoor living room," it was recommended that porches be furnished accordingly, and savored for their healthy doses of fresh air and views of nature. Porches were also handy as spill-over space from the living room, since most bungalows' interiors are entered directly through the front door into the living room. The deliberate interaction of this primary interior living space with its adjacent outdoor counterpart also helped to create the welcoming and informal impression for which bungalows are known. Once inside, the benefits of a shared feeling of space usually continued in maximized visual access between major rooms.

As the primary family gathering and entertainment space, every bungalow floor plan revolves around the centrality of its living room. The great majority feature a prominent fireplace often flanked by built-in bookcases or built-in seats (figs. 8, 9). When fireplaces were located on outside walls, it was very popular to place two matching windows above the built-ins on either side. Usually small casement windows that could open to provide ventilation, these added an additional source of fresh air and light for the interior. Strongly affecting the first impression one receives upon entering the house, the positioning of the fireplace was an important design consideration. Particularly desirable was a direct line of vision from the front door to the fireplace. When possible, this effect could be achieved most dramatically by a deliberate axial alignment

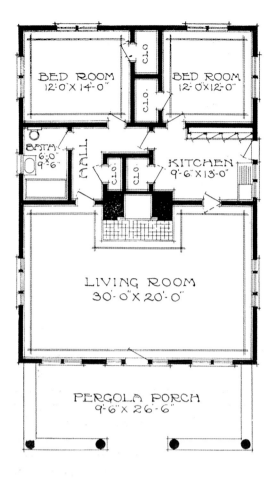

6. A bungalow floor plan. First published in Gustav Stickley's *The Craftsman* magazine in 1911 as "Bungalow No. 124," the article accompanying the plan and illustration of this one-story house gave an apt description of "a small, simply arranged dwelling, intended for a narrow lot, and planned economically to afford the greatest possible comfort within a limited space." Its thoughtful design manages to offset most of the limitations imposed by its scale, especially in the living room, which is at least as generous as those in much larger houses. Taking up nearly half of the total square footage of the house, this multipurpose room with an oversized fireplace embodies the bungalow-planning philosophy of making the space for primary living areas a top priority. The plan also incorporates two bedrooms of more than adequate size, and provides each with a generous closet. Minimal but functional, the kitchen and bathroom are conveniently central. The living room's generous scale could accommodate a large central seating arrangement around the fireplace, and still have space at the right for a dining area with a freestanding sideboard. At the left, and in the remaining corners, additional room is available for a piano, a desk, some bookcases, and a few extra chairs. Perhaps it was to assure its greatest flexibility that built-in furniture, expected in a bungalow, is omitted in this plan.

7. (Below) Exterior of the bungalow of the floor plan in figure 6. At lower right, this illustration bears Gustav Stickley's logo, the inverted U-shaped joiner's compass. Inscribed within is his adopted motto "Als ik Kan," the Dutch equivalent of "As I Can." Appearing in *The Craftsman* along with its plan, this appealing drawing of a modest bungalow with its garden setting and low-slung lines shows that Stickley knew his market well. In lieu of the more typical covered front porch, two pairs of sturdy columns form an open pergola supplemented by open trelliswork that forms a decorative screen for the plain façade. Softening its lines are climbing vines and other plantings promoted by Stickley to help the structure blend with its landscape. The proposed exterior wall surface was "cement plaster" or stucco, which Stickley recommended be left in its "natural" state, thus avoiding the endless maintenance cycle of repainting. Because of its expense today, many will be surprised to learn that slate was the original roofing material specified, and its exceptional long-term durability was probably the justification.

of the fireplace with the front door, placing it straight ahead as one enters the house (fig. 6). More typical was to locate the fireplace on one of the room's other walls, usually an outside one, enabling an immediate glance to the left or right upon entry to reveal the fireplace. To exaggerate their presence, many fireplaces were oversized, some with massive exposed chimney stacks or sweeping, room-wide mantels.

Even a small bungalow could be designed to accommodate the ultimate feature to enshrine the fireplace—an inglenook (fig. 11). Part of the bungalow mystique, this feature was marketed as the choicest spot for the family to be ensconced together in domestic bliss. Usually open to the living room on one side, the term specifically describes a fireplace recessed into its own alcove, with some kind of architectural separation from the rest of the room. By creating the effect of a room-within-a-room, an inglenook can also help to make the adjacent living room seem larger. Frequently outfitted with bookshelves, an inglenook by tradition should have built-in bench seating on either side of the fireplace. Descended from a medieval English stone fireplace also fitted with built-in seats, the term was occasionally given other names on original bungalow floor plans. An inglenook has been sometimes described as a nook, alcove, den, or even a smokery (perhaps suggesting some preferred uses of this feature). In lieu of being a separate space, an inglenook can also be created around a fireplace located at one end of a long, rectangular living room. In this arrangement, an enclosure of low walls, perhaps topped by a slatted wood screen or a pair of partial-height columns, was often used to separate the area.

In the most compact bungalow plans, a single, generously sized all-purpose room might suffice to accommodate both living and dining functions (fig. 6). However, the majority have a separate dining room, and somewhat surprisingly many also have a small, separate breakfast room. At the time these homes were built, the daily ritual of dining was a major family event, when not only each other's company was shared, but important household matters could be discussed with everyone present. Helping to combine the diverse family activities of the living room with those of the adjacent dining room was the use of a wide, wood-cased doorway opening between them. Incorporating low walls or built-in bookcases within the opening, at either side, was a typical arrangement. The rather elegant-sounding term colonnade was often used to describe a popular effect created by surmounting the doorway's low walls with squared, tapering columns. Sometimes this effect would be echoed, on a smaller scale, in the design elements of the dining-room sideboard (which might also be called a buffet, breakfront, or china cabinet). A standard and very practical feature found in most bungalows, these were sometimes located on a wall

adjoining the kitchen so that a pass-through opening could be incorporated. Dining rooms that featured projecting bay windows often made good use of this space by using it to support the built-in sideboard, or perhaps create a broad windowseat. Kitchen access from bungalow dining rooms was almost always directly through a swinging door.

The domestic kitchen in America was embroiled in an era of change when the bungalow became popular. Emerging electrical technology was rapidly addressing the needs of the average housewife, who was less likely than ever before to have servants to help her. The earliest bungalow kitchens tended to be small and often had a screened porch adjoining them to accommodate a laundry (figs. 8, 9). Sometimes an extra toilet was also provided in this area. The obsessive application of built-ins associated with other bungalow rooms was also found in the kitchen through multiple-doored cupboards and drawer units with tilt-out storage bins. Many kitchens sported the popular, freestanding Hoosier cabinets, which now seem almost like microcosms of the compact and practical bungalow-design approach. In a time when electric refrigeration was still being perfected, cabinets cooled by outside air—California coolers—were popular features for food storage. Stoves (also called ranges) were still the freestanding workhorses on legs that they had been for much of the Victorian period, and had recently made the switch from coal or wood to gas. The breakfast nook, developed in the bungalow kitchen, allowed a comfortable compact place for at least some family meals to be shared within the same room where they were prepared (fig. 11). This was good news for the weary housewife, whose early twentieth-century demands for fewer steps and greater convenience also helped the kitchen emerge as a center of family living much as we think of it today.

In terms of new technology as well as aesthetics, the development of the bungalow's bathroom in many ways parallels that of its kitchen. For both areas, the design requirements of durability, practicality, and ease of cleanliness were at the top of the list. Also starting out as something strictly white and utilitarian, the bathroom had evolved into something far more inviting (and even colorful) at the end of the bungalow era. Many baths boasted ingenious built-in units, some combining extra drawers and cupboards with a lift-up bench seat for a laundry hamper. Often placed between two small casement windows, a convenient source of good natural light and fresh air, a mirrored medicine cabinet above a pedestal sink was standard equipment. Most bungalows were built with only one bath, usually placed between or adjacent to its bedrooms for the greatest convenience (figs. 6, 11). When possible, economy dictated that it also be located in close proximity to the kitchen's plumbing supply (fig. 10). Most bungalow plans show a concern for shielding direct access to the

8. A bungalow and floor plan. The design of this house incorporates simplified Craftsman-style forms. Slightly flaring out at the foundation line, it has wide horizontal clapboard siding. One of the few vertical elements in this low-slung composition is the massive chimney, which appears to be stuccoed. Incorporating exposed rafter tails and larger projecting beams at its gable ends, the construction of the front porch gable matches that of the main roof. The interior layout of this house epitomizes the space-saving obsession that characterized bungalow planning. Probably dating from the mid-Teens, it appeared in a plan book called *Wilson's California Bungalow*, published by Henry L. Wilson. The projected construction cost was about $700, and the overall dimensions are only 31 feet wide by 20 feet deep. Most bungalows have very little separate circulation space, but this one has none, so every square inch is put to work. The floor plan requires that both of its major living spaces serve a dual purpose. This plan retains separate dining and living rooms to help supplant the lack of any bedrooms. Achieved through a classic bungalow-style use of some ingenious built-ins, its alternative bedroom solution was "disappearing beds" (abbreviated to read *dis bed*, with each indicated by a large dotted "X"). These pull-out beds were contained in a rolling, drawer-like enclosure. One such bed in the living room is incorporated in the lower part of a built-in desk unit. When not in use, it slid back under built-in drawers in an adjoining walk-in closet and below a built-in linen closet in the bathroom. The other bed is located beneath a built-in dining room buffet or sideboard and was also pulled out when needed. It slid back under built-in kitchen storage cabinets and a dresser that was built into a small dressing room. Like the large walk-in closet off the living room, this space had a window for airing one's clothes, and each afforded a vestige of privacy and personal storage in the absence of a separate bedroom. Another accommodation is the separate doors to the bathroom from the living room and dining room.

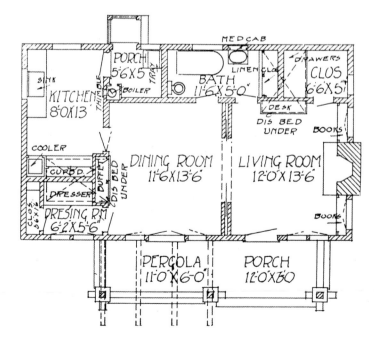

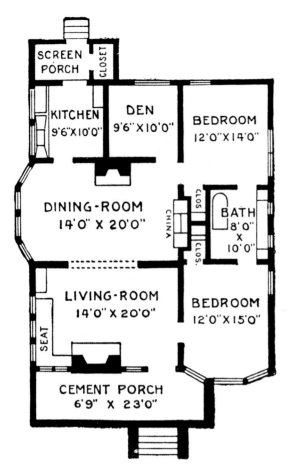

SCREEN PORCH · CLOSET

KITCHEN 9'6"X10'0"

DEN 9'6"X10'0"

BEDROOM 12'0"X14'0"

DINING-ROOM 14'0" X 20'0"

CHINA · CLOS.

CLOS.

BATH 8'0" X 10'0"

LIVING-ROOM 14'0" X 20'0"

SEAT

BEDROOM 12'0"X15'0"

CEMENT PORCH 6'9" X 23'0"

9. A bungalow floor plan. Designed by architect R.B. Young, this California house was published in *Modern American Homes*, a 1913 book by Hermann von Holst. This plan was submitted to the book by Pasadena architectural writer Helen Lukens Gaut, best known for her West Coast contributions to *The Craftsman* magazine. It is unusual that this bungalow has fireplaces in both its dining room and living room, and they are treated individually and not as a pair. On the front porch the chimney of the large living-room fireplace is featured as a prominent element of the front façade. Next to the living-room fireplace, the effect of a partial inglenook is created by a built-in bench that wraps around the corner. Most likely a bookcase, another built-in is indicated along the same wall. Generously sized, the dining room has a room-wide angled bay window and a built-in china cabinet on the opposite wall. To the left of the fireplace a door leads to a kitchen, well lighted by a pair of large windows. Set into one side of a counter below them, the sink has a pair of built-in drainboards on either side. The kitchen benefits from a built-in storage closet on the small screened porch. The separate den, entered from the dining room, was considered an extra amenity, although it was not as unusual as there being two fireplaces in such a small house. Two good-sized bedrooms are each entered directly from the two main living spaces. Placed back-to-back between the bedrooms are a pair of small closets, and a roomy, interconnecting bathroom that has a wide, built-in cabinet arrangement below the pair of small windows, which might have included a tall mirror, laundry storage under lift-up seats, cupboards for linens, and drawers for toiletries.

bathroom from primary living spaces, and tend to place it more discreetly off a small hallway leading to the bedrooms (figs. 6, 10, 11). In houses with attic levels developed into bedrooms, it was not uncommon for the only bathroom to be located on the second floor.

Most bungalow planning reflected an insistent air of practical philosophy, which recommended that the majority of square footage in a house should be given over to the primary living spaces. The reasoning for this enabled an otherwise smaller house to feel larger in those rooms where families gathered together or received visitors. This approach also minimized the square footage available for the kitchen and bath and frowned on any excessive circulation space, such as long hallways. It was almost as if every bungalow space was somehow required to justify its existence by way of maximum and sometimes multifunctional payback to its user.

Consistent with the approach seen in other private or utilitarian areas, the bungalow bedroom was generally conceived as a space for comfortable sleeping and dressing, with room for little else. The most typical floor plan has two bedrooms of similar size; the concept of the master bedroom didn't appear as we know it in the bungalow. However, the head of the household might have been inclined to lay claim to one bedroom over another if it

were distinguished by a bay window (fig. 9) or a better view. As a generous supply of fresh air was considered important for healthful sleep, most bedrooms had multiple windows (at least a double one), and a good closet was always provided. Many closets were actually quite large, and were sometimes equipped with built-in drawers. Instead of a traditional closet, some bungalows incorporated drawer, cupboard, and clothes-hanging storage units into walls that opened directly into the bedroom instead. A typical room arrangement placed the bath between two bedrooms, accessed by connecting doors from each, as well as one from the adjacent hall. While variations on bungalow bedroom and bath placement are numerous, they usually share a common practical approach that still works. Today, when considering remodeling or new construction, we can still learn many valid lessons from the ideas seen in original bungalow floor plans.

Popular tastemakers of the day repeatedly stressed in books and magazines that a simple home was a better home, echoing the famous quote of William Morris, "Have nothing in your houses you do not know to be useful, or believe to be beautiful." In this quest, along with the challenge of how compact a house could get and still be functional, many bungalow planners designed with the belief that the more built-ins there were, the less cluttering fur-

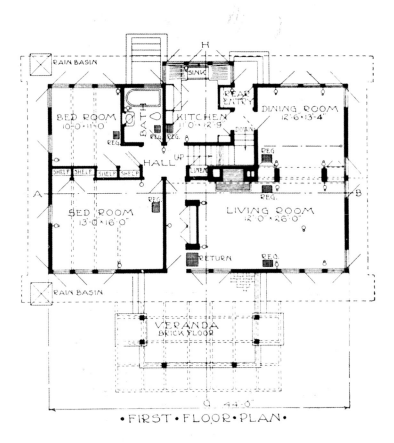

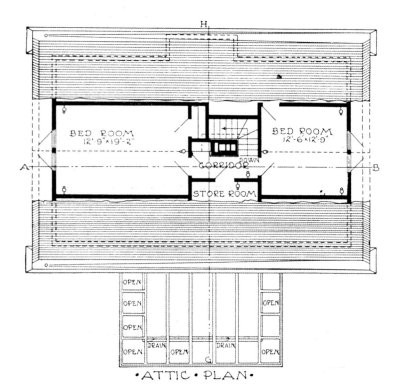

10. A bungalow's first- and second-floor plan. The house built to these plans was completed in 1909 for R.L. Blount in Tracy, Illinois, and its cost was approximately $4,000. Designed by noted Chicago architect Walter Burley Griffin (1876–1937), it shows influence of the Prairie School, a progressive early twentieth-century design movement that originated in the Midwest. Griffin was one of the early assistants of Frank Lloyd Wright. Working in Wright's Oak Park, Illinois, studio between 1902 and 1907, Griffin later achieved his own recognition by winning the important competition for planning the city of Canberra, the new capital of Australia, in 1911. That same year he married Marion Mahoney, a designer and draftsperson, who had worked in Wright's Oak Park studio for eleven years. Her distinctive drawing skills are seen in many of Wright's beautiful presentation drawings of this period. Hermann von Holst, another Chicago architect, included these floor plans in a compendium of recent domestic architecture called *Modern American Homes*, which was published in 1913. The exterior stucco walls of the house were left in their natural gray cement color. While the exterior woodwork elements were to be stained an olive green, the roofing shingles were to be "left to weather naturally." Its front porch veranda was designed as a screened-in outdoor living space, with its brick flooring set in a herringbone pattern, as sketched in a top right corner. Through open passages on either side of a large storage closet, an otherwise narrow entry hall flows directly into the living room at right. Not visible from the dining room, the living room's fireplace is immediately to the left of the entrance. The interior woodwork of the house was specified as oak in the main rooms and "pine in the service portion." Typical of Prairie-style houses, casement windows were used throughout and grouped at the corners for maximum light and air. The dining room connects to the living room through a wide opening that is flanked by built-in cabinets in an arrangement similar to the typical colonnade. Instead of the usual columns, narrow full-height wall elements are used in combination with these built-ins. The entire outside wall of the kitchen forms a squared bay window, which allows good light and ventilation. The window contains a wide sink with built-in drainboards. Near the center of the house, a pivotal hallway space connects with the entry, kitchen, bath, two bedrooms, and stairway to the second floor. Indicated in the two bedrooms at left are rows of dotted lines, representing the structural ceiling beams specified to be left exposed throughout the house, "thus giving greater height to the rooms." Passing a built-in linen cupboard on its way up, the stairs wind around a corner, reaching a short hallway on the second floor. Both of the upstairs bedrooms are larger than average. The peaked-roof house has side-facing gables; the shaded areas on the attic plan indicate storage or other undeveloped space. At the perimeter, the considerable overhang of the roof eaves is indicated by dotted lines.

11. A bungalow's first- and second-floor plan. J.S. Long, the owner of a construction firm called the Long Building Company, designed and built this Seattle house for himself. Soon after its completion, he submitted his house's floor plan to Gustav Stickley's *The Craftsman* magazine, where it was published in May 1916. Started in 1901, this influential magazine was then in its last year of publication due to financial problems for Stickley. Concurrently, the popularity of the Craftsman style was entering a period of decline, eclipsed by the Colonial Revival style that had been steadily gaining public favor in the housing market. Seeming to be almost grandly scaled, this house represents what could be done with a fairly modest budget at the time. The construction costs came to a total of only $3,350, including the $300 paid for the house lot. Immediately on entering the living room, a handsome ensemble of spaces presents itself. To the left, an inglenook as deep as the living room is raised up two steps. Its 9' x 12' size makes it a true room-within-a-room, and its large fireplace is the room's focal point. On either side of it, the usual arrangement of small windows above built-in bookcases are flanked by built-in benches. Above one seat, a grouping of three windows faces the street, while a smaller window across from it looks onto the outdoor pergola. On the opposite end wall of the living room a built-in windowseat is fitted into a projecting bay window. Accessible from the living room is one of the first floor's three bedrooms, which may also be entered from a rear hall. The living and dining rooms have different box-beam arrangements on the ceilings, which are indicated with dotted lines. The connected spaces of the dining room and outdoor pergola, which together suggest the effect of a three-sided courtyard, form the space around which all the other rooms are organized. A built-in sideboard or buffet is recessed into the far wall, and the rear hall is reached through a doorway to the right. The kitchen, larger than most, has several built-in features that are associated with bungalow design. At lower left, next to a built-in cupboard, is a cooler that is vented through the outside wall. Below three windows, the sink has a drainboard, and the countertop next to it has built-in bins and drawers below. At the far end of the room there is a compact breakfast nook or alcove. Adjoining the kitchen is a small utility porch and the back door. Providing access to the first-floor bedrooms and a bath between, the rear hall has two small closets designated for towels and linen. The closet of the corner bedroom features a built-in drawer unit. Up a straight flight of stairs from the rear hall, a second-floor bedroom, a generous sleeping porch, and a large closet are tucked beneath the highest gable of the house. Extensive undeveloped attic areas, to either side of these rooms, are mostly usable for storage, and are indicated by a dotted outline on the second-floor plan.

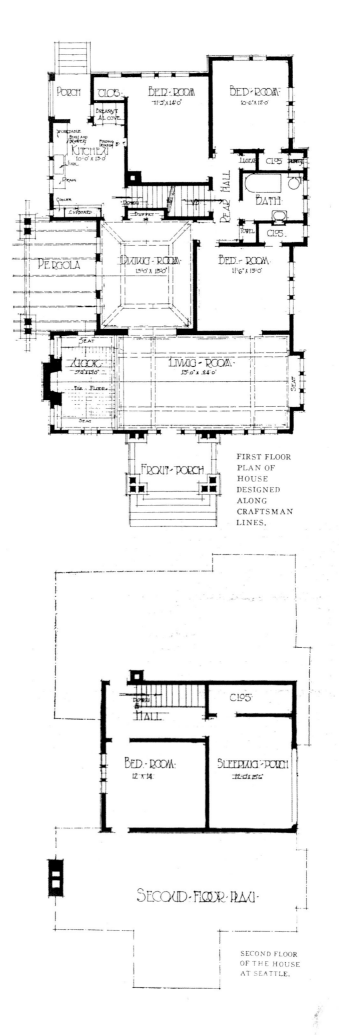

FIRST FLOOR PLAN OF HOUSE DESIGNED ALONG CRAFTSMAN LINES.

SECOND FLOOR OF THE HOUSE AT SEATTLE.

niture would be necessary. A trademark of bungalows became their built-ins, which seemed to be incorporated at almost every opportunity. Even the most abbreviated bedroom hallway was seldom without a stack of linen-storage shelves, each hidden behind a flip-down door with a spring-loaded hinge.

The simplest of bungalow plans might include only one primary all-purpose living-room space adjoining a kitchen and bath, much like the plan of today's efficiency or studio apartments. In plans this compact, more drastic space-saving arrangements were needed than those seen in the average bungalow. The popularity and wide availability of various kinds of mechanical "disappearing" beds, which were often indicated on original floorplans, made many of the most minimal floor plans workable as living spaces (fig. 8). While difficult for some to fathom today, it was essentially because of these miracles of modern convenience that bungalows without any separate bedrooms were able to be built at all, and still attract buyers or even renters. To offset this deficiency in such plans, a large closet, called a dressing room or "boudoir," would be provided to accommodate personal clothing and might, perhaps, also be outfitted with a handy built-in set of drawers. The remarkably diminutive scale of some bungalow plans recalls those seen in similar units of clustered "bungalow court" developments. Likewise, these plans suggest use by a single person, or perhaps a young couple, rather than as houses for family living.

One of those good ideas that wasn't new but highly promoted in the bungalow was the space-saving appeal of pocket or sliding doors. Thus unfettered by conventional doors, few features did more to enhance the feeling of flowing space from room to room. Most pocket doors were typically built of solid wood, and some incorporated glass panels to share light and views between rooms. Pocket doors also lent more flexibility to how rooms could be used. For example, it was not uncommon that the living or dining room would need to double as a guest bedroom. In addition to the use of the front porch, the living and dining rooms might temporarily expand into a smaller adjacent room otherwise used as a den or a bedroom. In some bungalow plans, with extra bedrooms in developed attic levels, a first-floor room that opened directly onto a primary living space might be labeled as a music or sewing room.

Fitted with multiple clear or frosted-glass panes, single-width French doors were also used extensively in many bungalow interiors. Occasionally, the use of operable windows between interior spaces was used to share both light and air. Many front or other exterior doors incorporated glass panels, and some were embellished with leaded and stained art-glass panels, often coordinating with similar designs on the glass-fronted cabinet doors of various interior built-ins.

Although the bungalow in general has always been popularly perceived as a modestly scaled house, there are some examples of a more generous scale that still manage to fit the definition of a true bungalow. These larger examples tend to have more than the typical two bedrooms found in the majority of single-story floor-plan arrangements, and many of them utilize their attic levels for additional sleeping rooms or other living space. Many bungalow attics yielded the easiest place to accommodate a sleeping porch (fig. 11), such as in a projecting dormer or at the end of an eave-shaded gable. Otherwise open to the outside air, sleeping porches could usually be enclosed by removable storm windows or screens and enjoyed a nationwide popularity for a time, comparable to that of outdoor camping. The sweeping rooflines of many bungalows also conceal a wealth of storage space in their tapering volumes, and attic bedrooms often have the largest closets in the house as a result.

A hallmark of most bungalow designs is a predominant feeling of ground-hugging horizontality. Yet, to fit on many minimally sized city lots, some bungalows were designed by necessity to go up more than they go out, and this variety was most likely to have some upstairs bedrooms. Others, with extra land to occupy, had an almost rambling quality to their floor plans. It is the more sprawling variety that were most likely to have multiple porches or pergolas. Such homes also tended to have the space for larger gardens.

Not as common were bungalows with central courtyard or patio plans. In colder climates, such houses were made more usable throughout the year and easier to heat by the use of a glass covering over the open courtyard, where a soothing water element might be found. Inspired by California's haciendas of Mexican or Spanish Colonial influence, this approach exemplified the interaction of indoor and outdoor space. Rooms could either face an intimate and private garden, or view an expanse of surrounding landscape. With direct physical and visual access to both of its garden environments, the courtyard plan epitomized an ideal of bungalow living.

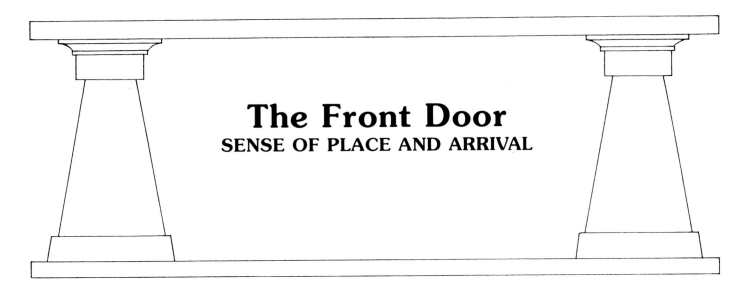

The Front Door
SENSE OF PLACE AND ARRIVAL

The emphasis given to the front door of a bungalow is significant. When in harmony with the overall design of the house, it visually rewards both visitors and occupants on a daily basis. As every home's ceremonial entry, the purpose of the front door is to accomplish an effective balance between the home's basic security and an aesthetically pleasing appearance.

The approach to any house comprises a sequence of impressions. Successively building on each other, these impressions reveal the character of the house. Establishing an individual sense of place, this passage from the street can be expanded to prolong the visitor's approach. Best when not progressing in a straight line, the path to the front door can sometimes be made to meander. A front garden's design (where possible) should suggest or reinforce the feeling of a natural landscape. Enjoyment of the passage to the front door can be heightened by the choice of paving materials, rocks, specimen trees, and seasonal plantings. It is also important to consider the sightlines of the return to the street, for the sequence of impressions should work well in either direction.

In light of the "outdoor living room" concept that was recommended for bungalow front porches, front gardens will also benefit from the same point of view, for the most successful gardens are those that appear fully integrated with the house. An invaluable source of inspiration is to be found in the design of small Japanese gardens. By the time one arrives at a bungalow's front door, one should be thoroughly infused with a sense of place. For a few moments before it is opened, the door's design and materials finally take center stage.

A major tenet of the Arts and Crafts Movement, which strongly affected the design of many bungalows, was concern about the appropriate use of materials. Particularly influenced by the Movement were houses conceived in the Craftsman style, so named and promoted by Gustav Stickley. The style was so strong an influence that, for a time, the terms *Craftsman* and *bungalow* almost became synonymous. Characteristic Craftsman design and detailing were best expressed through the prominence of structural forms, a use of natural materials, and a feeling of handcraftsmanship. The front door became one of the most popular ways that a bungalow could display an Arts and Crafts influence. Many doorways were unusually wide, and their broadness enhanced the feeling of welcome that greeted visitors.

Completely prefabricated and ready-to-hang front doors were part of the vast array of finished items that could be selected and purchased by mail through catalogs similar to bungalow-plan books (figs. 12, 13). Ironically, many of the front-door designs marketed in the Arts and Crafts style were, in fact, cleverly made by machine, so they were only intended to look handcrafted. From today's perspective, even front-door designs of this "dishonest" lineage may still be admired for how effectively their forms, finishes, and especially their hardware can still manage to evoke a feeling of handcrafting.

Unfortunately, many newer and often inappropriate front doors have replaced the original ones on otherwise intact bungalows. Choosing a proper replacement can be of real importance to restoring the overall success of the façade's design. Guiding this decision should be a concern that the character of the front door should always complement, but never eclipse or dominate, the overall design of the house. Before replacing a front door that is not original or causes doubt, one should locate and compare examples from as many similar houses as possible. Another useful resource for more examples of the period are publications about bungalows and reprinted plan books. Some sources may contain information about where to obtain a new door. One should also check with architectural salvage businesses for period doors.

Should it be necessary, the selection of an appropriate front screen-door design should receive the same care and consideration as the door itself. The quality of a front screen-door's hardware and finish should not be compromised by cost. Inasmuch as the original screen doors of bungalows had wooden frames, it is best to avoid metal, and to keep the designs and materials of both doors in harmony (fig. 40). When in doubt, it is always better to keep things simple. The most successful screen doors should almost disappear and allow the front door to make the primary design statement.

Particularly with examples of the Craftsman style, bungalows were encouraged to nestle comfortably into the landscape, and almost blend into it. Even when viewed from a distance and enshrouded in a natural setting, the front door of a bungalow may still be a significant element of its façade. In evaluating an existing front door, or when considering an appropriate choice for a new one, it is advisable first to consider the situation from the perspective of the street. Distance, scale, landscape, and other surroundings (such as the neighboring buildings) are all contributing factors, and should be taken into consideration.

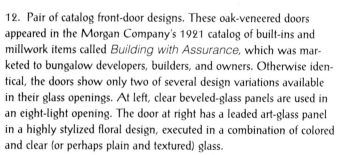

12. Pair of catalog front-door designs. These oak-veneered doors appeared in the Morgan Company's 1921 catalog of built-ins and millwork items called *Building with Assurance*, which was marketed to bungalow developers, builders, and owners. Otherwise identical, the doors show only two of several design variations available in their glass openings. At left, clear beveled-glass panels are used in an eight-light opening. The door at right has a leaded art-glass panel in a highly stylized floral design, executed in a combination of colored and clear (or perhaps plain and textured) glass.

13. A catalog "Dutch" door design. With its oak-veneer facing inset with many "butterfly key" inlays, this door was manufactured and marketed by the Morgan Company. Although the inlays were intended to evoke a hand-crafted detail that would actually strengthen the door's structure, the effect here was purely decorative. Fitted with clear beveled-glass panels, the door has a six-light opening in its upper half. The high placement of the door knob indicates that the door was divided in half—the familiar "Dutch" door design. The latch mechanism of the lower half is only visible from the interior, but was easily released from the outside, once the upper half was opened. The "Dutch" door was useful for providing fresh air while keeping small children inside the house.

14. Front door in Laurelhurst Park area, Portland, Oregon. One of the most popular door designs for bungalows, this period example is faced with quarter-sawn oak veneer, and has a single beveled-glass panel. The front doors of many bungalows have the familiar trio of squared-off corbels under a thick, shelf-like projection below the glass panel. This was probably a mass-produced door design, and its form and detailing appear to echo the typical high wood wainscoting and plate-rail arrangement found in many Arts and Crafts-style interiors. The polished brass hardware (marked Penn) has a handsome abstract geometric design that incorporates the circle of the lock into the over-all design. (For another view of this house see fig. 118.)

15. Front door in Long Beach, California. Located in the Rose Park Historical District, this 1913 bungalow's stylish, eye-catching front door has a flared casing, and its design is emphasized by the tapering outline of the single recessed panel. Equally unusual is the handsome, three-part leaded- and beveled-glass window. The distinctive outline of the door casing is repeated in the painted window frames of the house as seen at the left. Other original features include the Craftsman-style porch light, and the door hardware with its shield-shaped backplate. The recent (1996) designation of the Rose Park neighborhood as a new historic district was largely due to its treasure-trove of intact bungalow architecture. (For another view of this house see fig. 66.)

16. *(Opposite)* Front door near Seattle, Washington. Eminently suitable for a rustic 1910 log-built house, the four split planks used in this front door were made from tree trunks that were stained a pale gray-green. The planks are bolted into place with massive wrought-iron strap hinges, and a diagonal line of bolts secures an angled cross brace on the door's opposite side. The small window cutouts are fitted with panes of glass. The door is opened by lifting up the handle of its monumental door latch. (For another view of this house see fig. 36.)

17. Front door in Berkeley, California. This handcrafted door exemplifies the aesthetic approach of many Arts and Crafts designs. Three heavy cross braces span the wide vertical wooden planks, and they are secured together by heavy, artistically spaced iron bolts. Unlike front-door designs available from catalogs, this is an artistic, one-of-a-kind creation. The wood's naturally aged finish is set off against a weathered shingled wall of a 1906 rustic house in Berkeley's Scenic Park Tract. (For other views of this house see figs. 43, 71.)

18. Front door in Portland, Oregon. Displaying three massive, hand-wrought strap hinges, this door is not what it seems, for its show of hand-craftsmanship is a sham. The strap hinges are purely decorative (the real ones aren't visible), and the sturdy-looking bolts that appear to secure them are, in fact, no more substantial than large upholstery tacks. Nevertheless, its design is typical of many that were mass-produced and popular with the bungalow market. This home is in a northwest Portland neighborhood. (For another view of this house see fig. 25.)

19. Front door in Los Angeles, California. Here is another set of "sham" hardware that is affixed to the door just for its highly decorative quality and not for function. Such fancy hardware sets, which typically combined matching latch-set backplates with mock strap hinges, were popular with both homeowners and developers, and their designs were inspired by medieval English or Spanish metalwork. This Angelino Heights neighborhood has many notable historic homes dating from the early twentieth century. (For another view of this house see fig. 106.)

20. (Below) Front door in Spokane, Washington. This example of design bravado is found on a very modest but thoughtfully detailed bungalow, and serves to flaunt its front door like a beacon to the passersby. Belying its size, the door seems almost monumental, an impression emphasized by the elongated window openings and the extraordinary set of brass hardware, with its stylized oak leaf-and-acorn motif. This home is located in Spokane's South Hill neighborhood, which is especially rich in bungalow architecture.

21. (Opposite) Front door in Spokane, Washington. This impressive front door and flanking sidelights, topped by glass transoms, are a contemporary homage to the work of renowned American Arts and Crafts architects Charles and Henry Greene, architects of the famous Gamble House (1908) in Pasadena, California. Designed by the owner and builder, it was created for a recently completed house just outside Spokane, whose rambling design was only inspired by the Arts and Crafts style, rather than being an imitation. This door is both an emulation and an abstraction of the forms seen in the entrance to the Gamble House. The general disposition of its elements, although very similar, have a somewhat greater vertical emphasis here, as does the overall design of this house. Because of the complete absence of any art glass the interior of this house is flooded with light. Intended to recall the soft greenish color of the Gamble House, the shingles have been stained gray-green, translucent enough to let the character of the wood come through. (For other views of this house see figs. 37, 88.)

22. Front door (from inside entry) in Oakland, California. While the front doors of most bungalows open directly into their living rooms, the plan of this house accommodates a small entry hall, and allows its stairway to become a major design element. The wide front door at the left is fitted with a four-light casement window that can be opened. With the strong line of its top casing continuing around the room as a cap to the adjacent wainscot, the door is well integrated. The vertical rhythm of the board-and-batten-style wainscoting is repeated in the door's three recessed panels, and is complemented by the slatted, screen-like stair railing. A built-in bench at the foot of the stairs, with a lift-up seat for storage, and the stained-glass lantern are also original features. Built in 1910, it is one of many Craftsman-style homes built in the Rockridge district of Oakland during that period. (For other views of this house see figs. 28, 76, 90.)

23. Front door (from inside entry) in Spokane, Washington. Five wide fir planks create the form of this door that is made to appear wider by the matching fir of the door casing and wainscoting. Otherwise open to the living room, the ceiling's peaked form defines the small entry vestibule and is divided by shallow beams that support an original lantern. Even in the good company of Spokane's historic South Hill neighborhood, this 1907 home's near-original condition is still impressive. (For other views of this house see title page and fig. 46.)

The Fireplace
SYMBOL OF HEARTH AND HOME

In any house, probably more than any other feature, the fireplace has an intangible appeal. Gazing into crackling flames and feeling their radiant warmth can be a transporting experience, taking us away from our immediate cares to a timeless and nurturing state of mind. Fire symbolizes survival, sustenance, and shelter, so it is not surprising that a "place for fire" should have found its way inside our homes. Despite our diminished need for fire on a daily basis, the response to (and desire for) it has continued unabated, and it was inevitable that once fireplaces were built into houses (which is at least as long as people have been building), they would enjoy perennial popularity.

The bungalow, in America, has been inextricably linked to the fireplace, and a bungalow's modest scale heightens the prominence of its fireplace. There is also the undeniable influence of cozy vacation houses or mountain lodges with their mandatory roaring fires, which has colored our sense of association. The fireplace became prominent in bungalow marketing, and the public's deepseated attachment to fire was mercilessly preyed upon.

Bungalows without fireplaces are certainly less common, but they do exist. When excluded from original plans, it was usually due to economic reasons. It may not have been considered necessary, perhaps, because gas or electric heating sources were considered more modern and efficient. After all, these little houses long represented the wave of the future to many people. Some may have thought fireplaces to be impractical in areas with mild climates. In the smallest houses, built on the diminutive scale of those in the multiunit compounds known as bungalow courts, there literally wasn't room for one.

Helping to resurrect the emotional stature of the fireplace in the public mind today is the resurgence of interest in bungalows. The inglenook is enjoying a renaissance in bungalow interiors, for it is considered to be one of the coziest ways of enjoying a fireplace in one's home. Those who may be contemplating building a new bungalow should give serious consideration to including an inglenook in their plans.

The rich color and interesting texture of clinker brick have also been rediscovered. Clinker brick's appeal has always been to the more rustic side of bungalow design, which has also traditionally embraced river rock, field stone, and even cast stone. An interest in hand-built masonry has made a remarkable comeback in popularity, fueled by the current interest in log houses and the influence of Adirondack lodges, which are both known for their huge stone fireplaces.

The restoration and refurbishment of bungalow fireplaces has also ignited the ceramic-tile industry, which is producing an expanding range of tiles of all types, patterns, and glazes. It also is this field that is most connected to the revival of the Arts and Crafts Movement, for many of its artisans work as small businesses that specialize in producing hand-made or hand-finished tiles equal to the best of the period.

Many original fireplaces require special attention so that they work properly and safely; therefore, reconstruction may be necessary. If a smoke problem exists, it can often be helped or solved entirely by the addition of a small projecting hood, which often provides an excuse to have a handsome one handmade of beaten copper. Some fireplaces have been retrofitted to good effect with rather convincing concrete logs and gas flames.

The fireplaces that follow have their own individual character and reveal something of what hearth and home is all about. They also celebrate the richly varied legacy of Arts and Crafts design that is embodied in so many of our bungalows, which we must cherish and preserve.

24. Catalog fireplace and built-ins. Every conceivable built-in requirement of the bungalow interior could be procured from mail-order catalogs, as illustrated by this Morgan Company fireplace mantel design of 1921 for a library. Other elements also for sale are the bookcase units with leaded-glass doors and the pair of small casement windows on either side of the fireplace. Also typical of the Craftsman style are the tapering pilasters on the front of the fireplace. The river-rock facing on the fireplace and chimney was intended just as a design suggestion and was not part of the product line available by catalog.

25. Inglenook in Portland, Oregon. Strikingly symmetrical and slightly elevated for emphasis, one entire end of a generously sized living room is anchored by this commodious inglenook. Its separation from the rest of the room is formed by a pair of substantial columns mounted on low walls, which are attached to the right and left walls by screen-like slatted wood railings. Partially concealing one side of a stairway that is out of view at the left, similar slats form stepped sections of a screen wall treatment. Repeating the rhythm of the slats, two of Stickley's rocking chairs sit on the lively geometry of a Kilim rug. A vintage photograph of Crater Lake is mounted on a deep beam that spans the width of the room, and the lanterns hanging at either side, as well as those suspended from the living room's box beams, are original. The simplicity of the brick-faced fireplace is accented above the mantel by a shallow recess for display. Pillows and textiles from Afghanistan lend comfort and color to the inglenook's pair of L-shaped built-in benches. Creamy yellow walls and cheerful tailored curtains provide additional glowing color to the room. Designed by noted Portland architect Emil Schacht and built in 1925, this is a rather late example of the Craftsman style. Its renovation was completed by local architect Jimmy Onstott.

26. Inglenook in the Oscar Maurer house, Berkeley, California. Discreetly tucked into a living-room corner, this inglenook's placement allows visual access from either side of the wide doorway at right. Allowing greater flexibility, the pocket doors (shown closed) permit the use of this end of the living room for dining. The inglenook recess is paneled in fir and it incorporates a pair of shallow bookshelves above its full-width mantel. The fireplace and hearth are faced with the same mottled, matte-glazed tiles. The pair of small built-in benches are fitted with lift-up seats and substantial slatted arm rests. Overhead, hanging from intersecting box beams, is one of several matching lanterns that light the living room, which also features a high wood wainscot topped by a plate rail. (For other views of this house see figs. 2, 119.)

27. Inglenook in San Diego, California. This inglenook shows the influence of the Colonial Revival style, exceptionally popular in America, and which long outlasted the Craftsman style. Note the short classical columns that are similar to those on the front porch. The pair of built-in seats lift up for ample storage. With a rather small arched opening originally intended for coal, the handsome limestone-colored fireplace of pressed brick has both rough and smooth textures in its detailing. On its mantel of cast classical egg-and-dart and dentil moldings is displayed a collection of old Chinese sewing baskets. Wanting to use the original color scheme of the room, the current owner matched traces of the eucalyptus-green paint found behind the edges of some woodwork. Complementing this color is the pale gum wood used for the interior millwork, as well as the light shade of the maple floors. Built in 1906, the house is in San Diego's South Park neighborhood, close to Balboa Park. This is one of several neighboring areas bordering the park that have a fascinating cross-section of popular early twentieth-century housing styles.

28. Fireplace in Oakland, California. By its usual definition, because there is no physical separation from the rest of the living room, this fireplace with invitingly cushioned built-in seating is not really an inglenook. However, it is clear that several people could be readily accommodated in this very small space. The room's delightful warmth is enhanced by a high fir wainscot and plate rail that encircle its perimeter. The plate rail is unusually detailed with an overscaled dentil molding extending between occasional small wood corbels. Under the guidance of architect Glen Jarvis of Jarvis Architects, the fireplace was reconstructed to improve its draw and fitted with a new hand-made copper hood. At that time, the damaged tiles of its hearth (set flush with the oak flooring) and its facing were replaced with matching handmade ceramic tiles in a soft blue-green matte glaze. The owners hand-stenciled a stylized Arts and Crafts floral motif on Roman shades of linen, shown lowered over a pair of windows. Unlike typical box beams, which only imitate structural elements, the ceiling beams visible in this room are actually solid (4" x 10") Douglas fir joists, which support the floor of the bedroom above. (For other views of this house see figs. 22, 75, 90.)

29. *(Opposite)* Fireplace in C. Hart Merriam House, San Francisco Bay Area, California. When entering this house, visitors face this striking view. Directly opposite the front door and soaring to a remarkable height, the clinker-brick chimney of the fireplace dominates the scene. Just above the broad fireplace mantel, the brickwork begins to taper and then passes through the floor of the second-floor balcony, where the upstairs bedrooms are located. This all-redwood interior glows with rich natural color and forceful lines. The copper "hands" seen on the mantel were forms used in glove manufacturing. Although it seems quite dramatic, this house is rather modest in scale. It is sited near natural springs and dwarfed by a towering redwood grove. It was built in 1904 as a summer residence by C. Hart Merriam, a renowned anthropologist and naturalist, who is best known for his study and preservation of the customs and languages of native California Indians (particularly the local Miwok tribe). He was also an influential and founding member of the National Geographic Society and the Smithsonian Institution. (For other views of this house see figs. 90, 105, 114.)

30. Fireplace in Berkeley, California. An impressive construction in craggy clinker brick, this fireplace commands the living room of a rustic hillside house in the Scenic Park Tract. With an all-redwood interior, it was originally owner-designed and built in 1905. The recently created bronze smoke guard has two pierced quadrants of small squares (backed with mica) that are set aglow by the fire. Now supporting a pair of candlesticks, two projecting bricks were deliberately positioned to function as small shelves on either side of the fireplace opening. The top three rows of bricks form a high mantel shelf. Clinker brick, once discarded or sold as seconds, was prized by Arts and Crafts architects for its exceptional textural effects and rich color, which can range from blacks to deep reds to purple-grays. According to one account, the name *clinker* supposedly came from the "clinking" sound made when the bricks, placed too close to the kiln's heat source, began to burn and melt. Another theory states that the name is due to the sound made as the bricks were tossed onto piles of rejects or seconds. (For other views of this house see figs. 103, 104, 138, 139.)

31. *(Opposite)* Fireplace in Berkeley, California. In an elegant sweep of line, an original hammered-copper hood enlivens the opening of an otherwise austere clinker-brick fireplace. Terminating in the projecting courses of bricks, the design of the hood suggests an English Arts and Crafts influence. Darkly patinated metal straps are riveted to the copper, almost looking like great strap hinges. The fireplace is the handsome centerpiece of a peaked-roof, all-redwood living room in a 1908 house, which commands a steep hillside site. To utilize the site better, the bedrooms are located below the main living level. The Claremont Heights home was designed by the local architectural firm of Mallet and Chapin. The copper hood was crafted by D'Arcy Gaw, a woman architect and metalsmith, who shared a studio with the more famous metalsmith Dirk Van Erp in San Francisco between 1909 and 1911.

32. Fireplace in the Henry Weaver House, Santa Monica, California. Positioned opposite the front door for maximum visual impact, the most unusual feature of this broad, towering fireplace is the horseshoe-arch-shaped fireplace opening. This is a hybrid form of the rounded arch, and it is mostly found in Islamic architecture. The exuberantly figured woodwork of the fireplace is crotch-grained Tobasco mahogany, also well displayed across the ceiling in a series of box beams. Built in 1911 for retired hotel operator Henry Weaver, this bungalow was designed by the Milwaukee Building Company (later known as Meyer and Holler, who designed Hollywood's famous Graumann's Chinese Theatre). After severe damage from the 1994 Northridge earthquake, the house was sensitively reconstructed and restored by a team of experts, headed by restoration architect Martin Weill, under the auspices of the current owners. (For another view of this house see fig. 115.)

33. Fireplace in Seattle, Washington. Suggesting a Mediterranean influence, the contours of this plaster chimneybreast curl onto the ceiling, blending with the coved perimeter of the ceiling. The form of the fireplace, and prominence of the woodwork, is heightened by the use of a pale color against walls painted a deep terra cotta. A prized vase is set on velvet in the recessed niche. The original surround and hearth of matte-glazed tiles are in the picturesque style popularized by the work of Ernest Batchelder, and evoke the eclectic taste of the Twenties. Surface-mounted in a stepped configuration to create an interesting outline, scenic pictorial accent tiles are featured at the outer corners. In their diverse collection, the owners favor pieces of the English Arts and Crafts Movement, such as the embroidered screen at right. The carpet in this room was recreated after one of the Hammersmith designs by William Morris. The characteristic pair of small windows on either side of the fireplace lend additional light and balance to the far end of the living room, which opens to the dining room through an archway at right. Situated in Seattle's bungalow-rich Ravenna district, the house packs a lot into its compact plan, for both the attic and basement levels are fully developed.

34. Fireplace in Pasadena, California. This hidden treasure, found in the neighborhood designated in 1989 as the Bungalow Heaven Landmark District, is a California Arts and Crafts fantasy. On the broad horizontal panel, the early heritage of that state is evoked by a scene of the eighteenth-century Santa Barbara Mission, depicted in low-relief sculpture that is emphasized by the rough texture of the surrounding masonry. However, this is not a hand-sculpted example of Arts and Crafts artistry. It is a piece of clever foolery, developed for the burgeoning bungalow market and manufactured in cast stone (a type of concrete) by the Tay-mac Company. Nevertheless, the whole ensemble is both stunning and interesting.

35. Fireplace in Oregon City, Oregon. Reinforcing the predominant horizontality of the living room, the line of this fireplace's mantel extends across the top of the pair of built-in bookcases, as well as those that separate the dining room from the living room. The fireplace and chimney are completely faced with irregular pieces of slate-gray stone, actually a locally quarried basalt, which was possibly excavated on site during construction of this house. Mounted on a parallel beam is a trio of original lights that match several others mounted from beams elsewhere in this room and in the dining room. The house is filled with collectibles, and some of the most prized are the pieces of antique beadwork inside the glass-topped display table in the foreground. The house was built in 1910 on a bluff overlooking the Willamette River by the mayor of the town.

36. Fireplace near Seattle, Washington. Across an exceptionally deep fieldstone hearth set flush with the maple floor, the expansive yawn of this rustic fireplace's opening in a 1910 house of log construction invites one's approach. The irregular stonework recalls the informality and welcoming comfort associated with mountain lodges. Also evoking the hearty spirit of our Colonial-era hearths, its broad scale suggests that cooking, as well as sitting, could be accommodated. Stretching across the base of its tapering stone chimney, a split-trunk mantel and supporting log-end corbels are wonderfully appropriate fittings and repeat the forms of the log beams above. A bay window at right looks out into a densely wooded setting. (For another view of this house see fig. 16.)

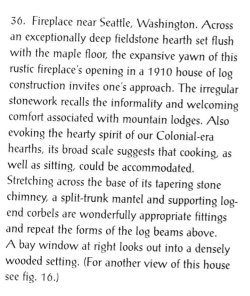

37. Fireplace in Spokane, Washington. This massive contemporary fireplace splendidly revives an American Arts and Crafts tradition of exploiting the softly rounded and randomly shaped qualities of river rock to express nature's beauty indoors. Two thick wooden shelves form a strongly horizontal termination to the stonework. Above them, the chimney continues its rise in full view past an open second floor landing up through the roof. The centrality of the fireplace organizes the open plan of the house into several zones. Use of interior doors is limited to the private and utility areas. The back of the fireplace is visible from the open dining room at the left. Leading to the entry hall and an open staircase visible behind the fireplace, the large opening to the right of the fireplace also leads to the master bedroom. No matter where one stands, bright light bathes this interior from virtually every direction, and the large expanse of glass that makes this possible also permits sweeping vistas of the surrounding countryside. The overall design of this house by Pasadena architect Doug Ewing handsomely fulfills its owner's wishes for a sensitive distillation of the Craftsman style. (For other views of this house see figs. 21, 88.)

The Living Room
HUB OF BUNGALOW LIVING

Bungalow designers were acutely aware that the living room was of prime importance, and they put an extraordinary effort into anticipating the impact this room would have on both the prospective homeowners and their guests. They knew that at the moment the front door was opened the room should be ready to cast its spell. Sure enough, not unlike the feeling of "love at first sight" between people, many homeowners confirm that they experienced much the same feeling when they first saw their own bungalow living rooms.

Conceived to address a variety of needs, the living room also had to function as a circulation space, for most bungalows didn't have the square footage to devote to a separate entry or hallway. More than most factors, this affected the arrangement of the furniture, for ease of movement through this room was a daily priority. No matter how modest the home, it was usually a high priority for households to be able to receive and entertain guests in comfort, and hopefully, with some degree of style. The bungalow living room was also the central place for the family to spend time together at home. With the exception of eating in the dining room or perhaps the kitchen, they would be in this room, or usually within sight of it. That meant it had to do "double duty" or better. By necessity, it was probably the most versatile of all rooms.

Whether in winter, by its warm fireside, or in the heat of summer, the living room was at the center of every conceivable home activity. Within its walls, important family matters would be aired and discussed. In its comfort, the latest books, magazines and newspapers were read and contemplated. It was here that the family gathered to listen to the phonograph and tune in their favorite radio programs. While sprawled across its floor, children spent endless hours playing board or card games. Music lessons

were dutifully practiced at an upright piano in this room. Young people self-consciously received or embarked on their first date through its portals. Now, as then, life goes on. It is probably more from our fascination with the past that "bungalow living" has been colored quite so appealingly.

In terms of their inherent features, many bungalow living rooms are simply blessed with "good bones." It may be a particularly stunning fireplace, exceptional woodwork, unusual built-ins, beautiful windows, a sense of good proportion, or a stunning combination of these that conveys this positive impression.

This is not to imply that even the best-designed living room cannot be improved upon. Chances are, in a bungalow, it is the only major living space there is, and it can also be a showpiece at the same time. But exactly how can it be improved, and at what cost? These are often the thoughts that occupy people's minds as they consider the purchase of a bungalow. The potential improvement of the living room is usually the most immediate and critical place to start.

Before deciding to change anything, spend some time in the room. A careful analysis of a living room's best attributes, perhaps even making a list of them, will help to evaluate what makes it work, and why. At the same time, a list should be made of every possible shortcoming the room may have. Bungalows, for all their touted flexibility, cannot be all things to all people. To love them is to understand the basic philosophy and approach to design that they express. For people who aren't familiar with living in an old house, it can be somewhat like learning a new language. Making any change is always a challenge to a bungalow's basic design integrity and cannot be too carefully considered in advance. The bottom line is to be as informed as possible and then to proceed with caution and care.

During the time of their greatest popularity, it was possible for bungalow homeowners to obtain decorating ideas and guidance from a whole range of design-advice books and periodicals. For those who were particularly drawn to the Arts and Crafts style, *The Craftsman* magazine was America's choice. In it, Gustav Stickley had the perfect forum not only for his own ideas, but also for those of architects, designers, and even do-it-yourself homeowners from across the country. Other magazines such as *House Beautiful, House and Garden,* and *Women's Weekly* were somewhat more mainstream in their marketing approach, and included the occasional Craftsman-style home, garden, or interiors along with those of the more conservative Colonial Revival style and some combinations of both. The early twentieth century was rapidly approaching the advent of the Modern Movement, which by the 1930s would supersede the popularity of and fashion for handwork and most ornament as being hopelessly dated. The public's love affair with bungalows and the Arts and Crafts Movement would be its victims.

Effective in concept and used to this day, the bungalow designers incorporated many handy built-ins. Originally conceived to reduce the need for other free-standing furniture, these can almost make an otherwise empty living room still seem lived in. Inglenooks were probably the ultimate built-ins. More typical was at least a bench or two, most often placed close (or physically attached) to the fireplace. Although not very deep, compact and used for occasional seating, built-in windowseats were also particularly popular. Built-in bookcases, usually with glass-fronted cabinets that might be fitted with art-glass panels, were found in a tremendous number of bungalows' living rooms, and were frequently placed to flank the fireplace or divide off the dining room. Bookcase and mantel units were also sometimes designed to incorporate a small drop-front desk unit, especially if no other study space was available.

Many of the functions the bungalow living room was designed to accommodate are still being handled very well today. While some people lament the lack of room for such staples of our era as stereos and television sets, even these problems can be dealt with. Some choose to relegate the television to another room, perhaps annexing a den or extra bedroom as a smaller version of the "family room" of contemporary homes. Others prefer to house electronic componentry in cabinets designed to fit into a Craftsman-style ensemble.

38. *(Opposite, above)* Design for a living room. Intended to showcase a fashionable use of paint, this color plate of a living room done in shades of green and reddish brown appeared in a promotional booklet published by the Eberson Paint Company. The form of the lower part of the fireplace with its broad, pale brick surround reflects a Colonial Revival influence, also seen in the pair of oval-backed, double-arm wall sconces mounted in the panel above. Built-in elements include the broad cushioned windowseat and in the corner an open-front bookcase. The room is lit by a Craftsman-style fixture hanging low from chains, and inset with stained glass. The table and two of the chairs are of the Craftsman style. Above the chair rail, which continues around the room, is a hand-stenciled border.

39. *(Opposite, below)* Living room in the Colonial Revival style. As the Craftsman style lost favor, painting a bungalow's woodwork white was one way to "colonialize" it, and this practice became increasingly popular in the Twenties. Published in the 1923 edition of *The Home,* an annual publication sent to subscribers of *Women's Weekly* magazine, this rendering allows us to glimpse a fashionable color and decorating scheme. A room-size carpet has a rich golden field set off by a figured border in a complementary shade of blue. Done up in Colonial Revival style, similar golden accents reappear in the fabric valance and tie-backs of the window treatment at right. The wallcovering, streaked in blue and gold, is probably intended to represent an embossed wallpaper. The rough texture of grasscloth, which traced its popularity to the Craftsman era, was originally considered a tasteful way to utilize the simple charm of a "natural" material as a wallcovering. Another wallcovering celebrated for its texture and simplicity was natural burlap, which also became popular in solid color (or color-tinged) machine-printed, imitation versions. Evoking a formal Georgian feeling are the red-brick fireplace and white mantel, while the box beams continue a favorite ceiling treatment of the Craftsman style. The narrow French doors at left indicate the ongoing popularity of direct access to the outdoors. Most of the furnishings are distinctly Colonial Revival in feeling.

39

40. Living room in Highland Park (Los Angeles), California. Seen through the wide front door at right, the "outdoor living room" or front porch spatially and visually interacts with this living room. Pieces from a collection of American Arts and Crafts furniture are used through-out both areas. Through the French doors at left is an enclosed sun porch that also doubles as a sleeping porch. Combined with both porch areas, this rather modestly scaled living room is expanded both in feeling and actual usable space. Unseen here are a built-in arrangement of a fireplace and bookcases at the right and the dining room at the left. Adding another source of ventilation and fresh air, a transom-like window can be opened above a larger window in the alcove area, which contains a Gustav Stickley settle.

41. Living room in Spokane, Washington. The box beams that crisscross this living room extend into the dining room at the left, and their intersections are punctuated by square Craftsman-style lanterns. With French doors visible beyond it leading to a den, a staircase wraps discreetly around a built-in bench at the right of the prominent brick fireplace. Most noticeable where the stepped chimney abuts one box beam, the fireplace is asymmetrically positioned in the overall space but centers on the primary seating group. Out of view is a built-in windowseat and bookcases on the wall directly opposite the fireplace. To the left of the brick fireplace with raised hearth is a slatted partial-height screen wall that contains an art-glass panel with a stylized landscape, and a duplicate of this screen wall is repeated on the other side of the wide doorway opening. The glass panel recreates the typical "storybook" stylization of landscapes so popular in art glass of the early decades of the twentieth century. Above the screen wall, a pair of doors in the dining room (the lighted one from the kitchen) is capped by a bracketed shelf, and these brackets are repeated above the wide doorway openings and below the mantel shelf. Built around 1910 and possibly designed by its original owner, the exterior of this South Hill area home its designed with a Swiss Chalet influence, one of several bungalow styles usually combined with some Craftsman-style elements.

(*Overleaf*) 42. Living room in Los Angeles, California. Shared vistas between rooms, to amplify their mutual feeling of space, was a typical bungalow design. Looking from the living-room fireplace, this view of the wide opening between living and dining room has a very characteristic arrangement of partial-height walls aligned here with the height of the adjacent wainscot, surmounted by short, tapering squared columns, and set below a room-wide dropped header (or beam). Partially visible on the far wall beyond are the china cabinets of the dining room's built-in buffet. Although favored for the effect of openness it allows, this screen wall also lends a feeling of individual identity and intimacy to either side. The wide pocket door at right opens into a den, which offers this floor plan the additional flexibility to incorporate this space when necessary. Under layers of wallpaper the owners discovered and were able to reproduce the original painted wall finish on sand-textured plaster. The richly colored textured finish combines a deep shade of blue-green over a mulberry color, which is reminiscent of the dull matte glazes and earthy color effects of Arts and Crafts pottery. The narrow drop-front desk below the picture of water lilies is an exact reproduction by Brian Scot Krueger of a rare 1901 design by Gustav Stickley. This room is in one of many classic bungalows in the West Adams district. (For another view of this house see fig. 68.)

43. Living room in Berkeley, California. Emphasizing the commodious seating both in the bay window and to the right of the fireplace, thick cushions and plenty of pillows in a tapestry fabric similar to designs of William Morris offer sofa-like comfort, not typical of most built-in benches. This seating area with its inglenook-like arrangement is only part of a larger space that serves as a multipurpose living room. The massive fireplace design closely resembles that of some very convincing cast-stone examples, popular with the bungalow market, which were sold in kit form, shipped in numbered pieces, and assembled on site, following a diagram. With walls and ceilings entirely constructed of Douglas fir, the main living areas of this house have a decidedly rustic, lodge-like quality that is very appropriate in its woodsy hillside setting. The house may date to 1906, and it was later owned and occupied (from 1935 to 1940) by the famous American photographer Dorothea Lange, who used its basement level as her darkroom. (For other views of this house see figs. 17, 71.)

44. Living room in Los Angeles, California. Viewed through the glass-faced front door of a 1906 house, this living room bids a warm welcome. Framed in boldly horizontal lines, a broad frieze area still awaits the replacement of the original early twentieth-century wall-paper, which was discovered by the owners during the removal of many subsequent layers of paper. Enough of the stylish, large-scale pendant frieze survived so that it could be adapted and reproduced by Bradbury & Bradbury Art Wallpapers. The paint colors of the room were matched to the originals found under the wallpaper. Faced with a thin and linear brick, which is sometimes called Roman, the fireplace features seven brick corbels that support the thick wooden mantel shelf and its display of pottery. The exceptional copper fireplace hood, which has applied designs resembling a pair of winged mythological beasts, is an artfully worked original treasure. Also original are the ceiling fixture and the pair of sconces mounted on the brick facing of the fireplace. The five pieces of Gustav Stickley furniture are made of mahogany. Other distinctive Craftsman-style pieces include the tall-case clock and the folding screen at the left with its original burlap and wood lattice work. The pocket doors visible behind the screen lead to the dining room. Designed by local architects Hudson & Munsell, this home is one of many such treasures in and around the West Adams district. (For another view of this house see fig. 58.)

45. Living room (and looking into dining room), Berkeley, California. Exemplifying the expansive effect of flowing spaces and shared vistas between rooms, this living room is open to the dining room through generous open pocket doors. The dining room has a good view of the living-room fireplace and built-in bookcases, which are centered opposite the wide doorway. While both rooms enjoy considerable natural light, the center pair of operable French doors in the dining room (flanked by two fixed ones) allows a view of greenery and direct access to a small loggia (a terrace, recessed into the side of a building, and open on one side). Reflecting the different proportions of its window arrangement, a very low wainscot in the living room that aligns with the windowsills accents its greater feeling of horizontality. Light enters this room through a large, three-part window, and it is diffused by two sets of curtains. The sheerest set is fitted within the window casings. Facing into the room, more substantial curtains of a creamy linen have been hand-appliquéd and embroidered with a period Arts and Crafts design. Using a variation on sponge-painting, the room's warmly colored walls and ceiling were rag-painted, a technique that uses a tightly crumpled cotton rag to apply textural and color effects evenly to the entire surface.

47. Living room in the Charles Warren Brown house, Santa Monica, California. An early city-council member and local architect, Charles Warren Brown designed this house as his own residence, and had it built in 1908 on a corner lot in the Ocean Park district. Now one of Santa Monica's oldest neighborhoods, at the time this house was constructed it was an unincorporated area of mostly beach houses. Entry to the living room is through the front door at right. On the floor at the right is a rare Native American Two Gray Hills rug. The two-tiered form of the fireplace that is faced with sturdy paving bricks makes an effective pedestal for a long candelabrum, which was fabricated from stray drapery hardware. The hand-crafted fireplace screen was recently commissioned for this room, and the set of fireplace tools was once owned by President Franklin Delano Roosevelt, and used in the house from which he broadcast his famous radio "fireside chats." Pieces in the owner's Arts and Crafts collection that are seen in this room include the Tiffany "turtle-back" Zodiac lamp on an open music stand designed by Harvey Ellis (at the left of the front door) and an early Gustav Stickley trestle table on which is a copper-and-mica Dirk Van Erp lamp (at the left of the fireplace). There is a Gustav Stickley #222 settle (in the foreground) and one of his drop-arm, spindle-side chairs in the far corner. The L. & J.G. Stickley rocking chair once belonged to the Stickley family. The small hanging lanterns are reproductions of a Harvey Ellis design, and the floor-standing reading lamp has been reproduced to a design by Gustav Stickley. The central ceiling fixture of bronze and stained glass is an early twentieth-century design made in Amsterdam. (For other views of this house see figs. 96, 97, 99.)

46. (Opposite) Living room alcove in Spokane, Washington. Helping to make it feel more expansive, this alcove is completely open to the rest of the living room, yet it also has some of the intimacy of a separate room. From its well-integrated windows, the view is across the front porch to greenery and an enormous boulder in the front yard. A strong architectural statement is made by the surrounding woodwork, in which the frieze area of each wall is framed by wood moldings. Almost miraculously, an original wallcovering of 1907 with a heavily textured leather-like embossing survives intact in the multiple panel insets of the high wainscot. At the left, above a tall Roseville Pottery vase, an original hammered-copper wall sconce (one of several) lights an outside corner. Resembling the pale tones and texture of parchment, subtle sponge-painted finishes have recently been applied to the frieze panels and the ceiling. The pair of chairs and ottoman of recent vintage recall that Gustav Stickley and others recommended the use of sturdy wicker designs as being appropriate for almost any room of a Craftsman-style interior. (For other views of this house see title page and fig. 23.)

48. Living room of the Frank C. Hill house, Los Angeles, California. This living room enjoys direct access to a raised garden terrace, which is elevated from the street because of a sloped building site. Its all-redwood detailing and finish are of exceptional quality and sophistication. The doors and windows throughout the house have the same single cross-bar detail near their tops. The subtle and extraordinary design of the brick fireplace, with its hand-carved sculptural panel, is centered between two pairs of casement windows. Below each, abutting the fireplace, are roomy built-in seats, fitted with thick cushions. There is also a small den, open to the living room through a wide doorway just out of view to the left, which has another fireplace and a built-in seat. In typical bungalow fashion, the house has only two bedrooms, but it is far more luxuriously appointed than the basic plan-book designs. Known by the name of its first owner, this exceptional bungalow was built about 1911 and designed by the local architectural firm of Vawter and Walker, who were in partnership between 1910 and 1916. Of the two partners, it was John Terrell Vawter who is believed to have been the most creative force. Before relocating to Los Angeles, he had worked briefly with noted architect Emmor Brooke Weaver in San Diego, and had developed a feeling and facility for designing small but special wooden houses. The floorplan and one exterior photo of this house were published with an article on Vawter that appeared in the important catalog to the exhibition, *California 1910* (published in 1974), which was early and influential in reawakening public interest in the American Arts and Crafts Movement as it related specifically to California.

49. *(Opposite)* Detail of fireplace in the Frank C. Hill house, Los Angeles, California. A delightful surprise, the hand-carved, low relief panel above this fireplace makes other brick chimney facings seem underutilized. An original work of art, it was executed by John Stanbough Souther, who signed it in the lower left-hand corner. The scene carved into the brick depicts a pipe-playing figure on a sylvan hillside. The fireplace opening retains its handsome, original copper-and-steel hood. After sustaining considerable damage from the 1994 Northridge earthquake, all of the components of this fireplace had to be numbered, dismantled, and reassembled. Consistent with the idea of bungalow living oriented to nature, within the walled enclave of this house can be found generous garden areas, and even an orchard, all of which enhance the illusion of a private Eden.

51. Living room in Seattle, Washington. Upon entering this room, visitors see at once the original and unusually wide stone fireplace and a long view into the adjoining dining room at left. Rescued by its current owners from years of neglect and misuse, the new design work for the extensive renovation was done by The Johnson Partnership, a local architectural firm. Shallow box beams, which traverse the ceiling and align with the width of the fireplace, had to be recreated. The stonework of the fireplace, which had been stuccoed over in a previous ill-advised attempt to modernize the house, had also sustained some structural earthquake damage. In restoring it, the architects added the gray keystone at its center, and took the opportunity to have the home's construction date of 1909 carved into it. Adding to the warmth of the room are its board-and-batten wainscoting, which continues across the top of the mantel, and the seat which is built into a deeply recessed window. Appropriate period lighting includes the pair of brass and stained-glass wall sconces above the fireplace, and Handel table lamps. The room contains notable furnishings by Limbert, including a large settle at left, an octagonal table with cut-out legs, and an early armchair with its original leather by the fireplace. Its embroidered pillow from the period is one of many designs that were sold in kit form, with a traced design and yarn provided, to be worked and finished at home. Similar kits are available and popular again today, further evidence of the Arts and Crafts revival. (For another view of this house see fig. 72.)

(Overleaf) 50. Living room in Los Angeles, California. Refinement abounds here in the warm red glow and restful lines of the Honduran mahogany woodwork. Upon closer inspection, some of the detailing reveals a trace of Greene and Greene influence, particularly the use of contrasting square ebony pegs, which are set into the corbels supporting the fireplace mantel shelf. Executed with a refinement more typical of fine furniture than interior millwork, other details include a repeated use of a flattened bracket-like element, with a single ebony peg, at the tops of the vertical door and window casings, and above the fireplace. A pair of hand-carved panels in the columns supporting the mantel incorporate an unusual vertical variation of the Greenes' familiar "cloud-lift" motif, which they had derived from traditional Oriental designs. A small hand-hammered copper hood harmonizes with the color of the Grueby fireplace tiles. The arrangement of the ceiling's elegantly detailed box beams, which frame a large central panel, surround it with smaller ceiling panels, all painted a deep blue-green. The homeowners, Joe Ryan and Chuck Roché, have assembled a significant collection of Arts and Crafts furnishings to complement their home. Chuck painted the two California landscapes displayed in the left corner of the room. The wide doorway leads to a den/library, and features substantial pocket doors, faced with mahogany on the living room side, and quarter-sawn oak on the library side. This 1911 house was built by local architect/builders (and brothers) John and Daniel Althouse, in the West Adams district that is adjacent to the University of Southern California campus. (For another view of this house see fig. 59.)

52. Living room in San Diego, California. A repository of many Arts and Crafts treasures, this room has many classic bungalow features. Its sense of space is expanded by its view of the dining room beyond. Between them, a room-wide doorway is framed by a pair of built-in cabinets (one visible, facing inward), whose tops form convenient display surfaces. The fireplace wall is fully developed with built-ins, including a bench on the right side, and a bookcase with leaded-glass doors on the left (now housing a fine collection of pottery). The unusual ceramic tile of the fireplace facing and hearth is original, and it is made up of strongly mottled, matte-glazed tiles in deep blue-greens. Orangey-brown highlights in the glaze help to relate the tiles to the color of the surrounding gumwood. To the left of the fireplace opening that is spanned by a shallow, hand-hammered copper hood, a Gustav Stickley coal bucket rests on the tile hearth. In the Craftsman taste, the use of boldly patterned and colored textiles of Native American designs enlivens the floor and adds comfort to the furniture. In the Mission Hills neighborhood, the house dates from the late Teens, and is in an enclave of many well-preserved bungalow homes of similar vintage.

53. Living Room in Pasadena, California. An example of the Craftsman style at its sleekest, the spare lines of this room still satisfy and come together handsomely in the fireplace wall. Revealed as one steps through the front door and glances to the left, the brickwork is detailed with a wseries of recessed panels that are well proportioned in their horizontal space. The divisions in the glass-fronted bookcase doors restate the feeling of linearity in the brick design. The fireplace mantel runs the full width of the room in one sweeping line. The pair of casement windows above it are linked to their neighboring windows by a continuation of their upper casings and further unify the room's design. A U-shaped bungalow in plan, the band of windows at right open onto a small courtyard or patio. Profuse light enters the room from three sides and boldly dispels the myth that bungalows have to be dark. Built in 1911 in the Oak Knoll neighborhood, the house plan was from the Sweet Bungalow Company. Enlisting the skills of Elder Vides of Painting Concepts, its current owners recently completed an extensive restoration of the house. Another distinctive feature is a pair of matching sleeping porches projecting off the back bedrooms, which form a secondary U-shape oriented to the backyard. The cushioned Craftsman-style furnishings are all examples of recent Stickley reproductions and adaptations. The broad-armed settle in the foreground has an architectural presence well suited to the lines of this room. (For another view of this house see fig. 113.)

54. Living room in West Linn, Oregon. Adapted from a plan for a "two-story country bungalow," first published in Stickley's *The Craftsman* magazine in October 1909, this room is in a house built in 1988 that successfully demonstrates what can be done with new construction today. Planning to build a new home, the owners consulted some of the reprinted plan books, and fell in love with this particular plan. They commissioned Portland architect Jimmy Onstott to adapt it for them, which required reversing the orientation of the room arrangement, to make better use of their site. Reversing plans was common practice at the time, and was a usual option offered in bungalow plan books. Probably the most striking feature of the house is this unusually large living room placed at the center of the house and which opens to the outdoors at either end. The plan conveniently organizes the first floor into three distinct zones: living and dining in the center, kitchen and utility spaces on one side, and two bedrooms and a bath on the other. The living room is dominated by a huge fireplace (if not the one with a five-foot-high opening that Stickley called for). Devised by Onstott, the facing shows at its outside corners an ingenious combination of brick merging with a native local stone. A stone "grille" fosters ventilation, and the opening is fitted with impressive hand-hammered wrought-iron doors. The doorway at right leads to the kitchen and outside. Mostly converging around the fireplace, the owner's furnishings are a comfortable mix of rustic, Arts and Crafts, and contemporary leather seating. One of the most appealing features of this room is its natural lighting. A design comprised of two layers of massive beams against an all-wood ceiling provides a surprising light and airy effect.

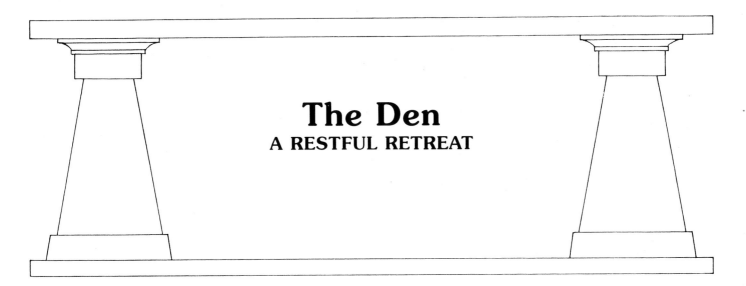

The Den
A RESTFUL RETREAT

The auxiliary living space frequently described as a "den" in bungalow-plan books might also be aptly described as the "chameleon" of its rooms. With the potential to accommodate almost any activity that needed a separate space, it was usually located close to or directly adjoining the living or dining room, and its central placement was an indication of its intended flexibility. While not every bungalow was blessed with one, such an extra room is remarkably common in many plans of modest scale.

Much like the term *bungalow*, a den's specific definition can be confusing. One reason is that usage of the term in many plan books is inconsistent. Dens appear on different floorplans and sometimes describe spaces that don't necessarily resemble each other. For example, the term may be used to describe an alcove (perhaps with built-ins) open to the living room. Some plans prefer to label an inglenook (with a fireplace) as a den. Depending on its intended audience, what might otherwise be described as a den might conceivably be labeled a music room, or perhaps a sewing room. Even a breakfast room on one plan could be interchangeable with the den of another similar plan (fig. 9). Some simply prefer using the terms *study* or even *library* to describe such spaces and avoid using den altogether.

No matter what they might be called, the majority of dens were intended as retreats from the activities of the rest of the house, for the concept of "quiet time" was valued as much then as it is now. In fact, the deliberate inclusion of such areas in many floorplans supports the popular reputation that bungalows garnered as being progressive houses that addressed real human needs.

Whether writing letters, keeping household records, or paying bills, such activities tended to make the den into a working study, where one could find a calm and private atmosphere. It is common for many bungalows to have some kind of built-in provision for accommodating paperwork, most typically a drop-front desk that is part of a larger ensemble of cabinetry or shelving (figs. 58, 59).

Reading, and the accommodation of books, was one of the most popular uses for dens. Sometimes the arrangement suggests a "den/library." Prior to the advent of radio and television, people simply read more books, for reading was perceived as an ideal pastime. Built-in bookcases were prominent bungalow features, but they didn't always get put in locations that invite a quiet interlude of reading. Most bookcases were placed in the immediate vicinity of the living room. The presence of some bookcases in an otherwise secondary room is probably the surest way to confirm that it was originally intended as the den.

Decorative taste notwithstanding, few people living in bungalows today are troubled by what is the proper way to use their den. In a compact house it can be a godsend, for there are many uses that go beyond those outlined or illustrated here. Dens can also be a nursery or child's bedroom, as well as a reasonably good (if snug) playroom. Some are used as small TV or family rooms, and can convert to a guest room when needed. Its changeable nature is another indication that the bungalow is as flexible as ever.

55. Catalog built-in desk and bookcase. Placing an order for this built-in unit, which was illustrated in the Morgan Company's catalog of 1921 called *Building with Assurance*, would result in an instantly outfitted den, study, or library, depending on what the household chose to call it. Not only useful for book storage or display, this unit also incorporates a small personal workspace, probably best suited for correspondence or household bills. Many such units or variations of them made their way into bungalow dens and sometimes living rooms. Less typical is the unit for storing books below the built-in windowseat, another item sold by Morgan. The leaded-glass doors on the large unit were considered an upgrade; the use of plain glass was more usual.

56. *(Below)* Design for a den. This illustration for a linoleum advertisement appeared in major shelter magazines in the Twenties. The decorative approach as seen in this den is what most would call masculine taste, for instance, the model sailing ship, the map on the wall, and even the drafting-table setup. Fashionable middle-class taste is seen in decorating touches: the coordinating textiles of the draperies and upholstery, the pillows on the built-in windowseat, and the hooked rug under the stool at the desk. Linoleum was promoted as being suitable for almost any room of the house, and this pattern was one of many that imitated ceramic tile. Except for the large rattan easy chair, most of the furniture is Colonial Revival in style (seen in the turned legs), which was very much in fashion when this advertisement was published, for by the Twenties, the popularity of the Craftsman style was in its decline.

57. Den in Pasadena, California. Located at the back of the house, this den has a pleasant view of the garden through a French door, which leads to a brick patio area. At the right, an art-glass window opening onto a utility porch provides an additional source of light and ventilation. The effect of a high wainscot is simulated by the vertical fir battens that are placed directly against the plaster wall and capped by a wide casing. At the left is a dark-stained free-standing bookcase with leaded-glass cabinet doors. The small writing desk and bookcase at the right are by Gustav Stickley, and the rocking chair is by L. and J. G. Stickley. The house is one of many that have been revived, along with the esteem of the entire neighborhood, in the Bungalow Heaven Landmark District.

58. Den in Los Angeles, California. The unusual high coved ceiling lends airiness to this well-appointed den, which retains its original 1906 gas fireplace heater insert that is designed to resemble a small log fire. It is incorporated into a built-in wall unit, below a plain wood panel and chunky mantel shelf, where pottery and an Arts and Crafts clock are displayed. Framing it are two-part built-in bookcase units, which have plain glass doors in the lower portions. Above them, the smaller units feature nine-light leaded-glass doors, with purposely irregular leading to suggest age or quaintness. At the right, a full-size built-in desk sits in its own recess. Its upper portion, flanked by small drawers, is also fitted with a drop-down panel that conceals an assortment of cubbyholes. The paint colors match the original ones discovered in the adjacent living room. An aura of comfort is ensured by two period Morris-style chairs, and with some additional color supplied by a few Oriental rugs. (For another view of this house see fig. 44.)

(Overleaf) 59. Den/library in Los Angeles, California. In the wall of built-in bookcases and a desk that spans one end of this splendid room, the quarter-sawn oak woodwork is a stylish homage to Greene and Greene. The divisions in the glass-fronted bookcase doors are variations of the Greenes, "cloud-lift" motif, and around the top of the wainscot, each corbeled bracket is accented with three square ebony pegs, and similar pegs are set at either side of the slant-top desk that has a display shelf for pottery. Well-integrated into the wainscot, the door in the corner opens into a separate breakfast room. Possibly the most exceptional feature of the room is its original frieze. Dating from 1911, it is made of a machine-printed and embossed paper, which was made to simulate antique tooled leather. It was probably made by M.H. Birge & Sons Company of Buffalo, New York. This pre-finished material should not be confused with Anaglypta or Lincrusta (other popular, but less expensive, embossed wallcoverings), whose painted finishes were always applied on site, after the material was installed. With new iridescent glass shades, chosen to match a single surviving example, the original shower-type light fixture still lights the room. (For another view of this house see fig. 50.)

60. Window alcove in Seattle, Washington. Open to a living room at the left, this alcove is created by a wide bay window. The splendid light admitted through its many-paned windows brightens the living room, and a pair of built-in seats are placed at either end of the bay window, each being partially concealed behind low slatted screen walls. So named because it was originally designed to fit above an upright piano, the wall space at the right features a high, horizontal "piano window." It now accommodates a small desk. In this 1910 bungalow a wide inglenook on the opposite wall of the living room duplicates the proportions of this bay window.

61. (Below) Den/Library of Mariposa (formerly the Frost-Tufts house), Hollywood, California. Designed in 1911 for Dr. C.L. Frost by architect Arthur R. Kelly, the original floor plan labeled this room a bedroom. Suggesting that this area was perhaps Dr. Frost's private domain at home, a small adjoining room (labeled laboratory on the same plans) is located off the opposite end of this room and also has access to an outdoor terrace. This room was made into a den/library by current owner and film producer Monty Montgomery under the guidance of restoration architect Martin Eli Weill as part of recent major work on the entire house. While the adjacent first-floor areas have natural woodwork, this room's woodwork, including the board-and-batten ceiling, was painted for the current scheme. Covered with natural burlap and framed by cream-colored walls and ceiling, the original treatment of the frieze area has been recreated. Stereo speakers are discreetly concealed behind the burlap. The built-in cabinet and drawer unit at left contains home-entertainment units and other storage. The wall at right has built-in open bookcases with enclosed storage cabinets below and indirect lighting above. A scattering of Navajo rugs brings color and bold geometric patterns to the room. (For other views of this house see fig. 98 and figs. 84–91 in *The Bungalow*.)

62. Den/Library in Berkeley, California. Outside the French doors of this room is a winding street in the Scenic Park Tract, where the first phase of this house designed by an unknown architect was built around 1912. This room is part of the second phase of construction, which didn't occur until 1921, when noted Berkeley architect John Hudson Thomas designed this addition, which extended the house toward the street. A massive bracket with a chamfered edge (one of a pair) frames a large recessed wall panel. Original and well preserved, the intriguing mottled texture of its painted finish is also seen in the panel above the desk and on other small wall areas in the room. Its effect was intended to add a feeling of age to the room, and combined with the bracket's design indicates the emerging popularity of historic-revival styles that dominated the Twenties. Not seen in this view are more large brackets that are grouped in pairs and arranged around built-in bookcases. A narrow bookcase wraps tightly around the corner next to the desk.

(Overleaf) 63. An "ingle-den" in San Diego, California. In a humorous term intended as a combination of an inglenook and a den, the dual identity for this room is invoked. Raised up a step and open to a front entry hall, this disarmingly compact room beckons with a clinker-brick fireplace. In front of it, a child's rocker and stool contribute to the slightly confounding sense of scale. Influenced by the Colonial Revival style, the doorway's elements are arranged in what was sometimes called a colonnade, most typically used to separate primary living spaces, while retaining visual openness. This alcove-like room is set off on its own, which suggests it was a retreat from the activities of the living and dining room. A single built-in bench runs the length of the right wall below windows that look out to a side yard. With its abundance of storage for books to peruse, and a smattering of interesting textiles and other collectibles (including a restored antique phone) to admire, the original early twentieth-century atmosphere of this "ingle-den" comes alive.

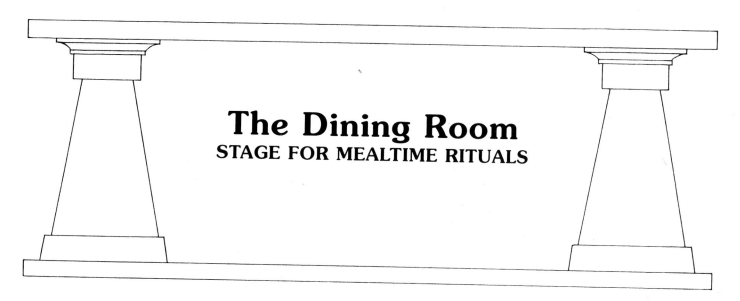

The Dining Room
STAGE FOR MEALTIME RITUALS

Second only to the living room in importance and use, the scale of the bungalow's dining room may seem disproportionately large. There are several reasons for this, some of which are related purely to design and planning issues, and others that reveal much about American family life in the early twentieth century. If the living room was the heart, the dining room could be aptly described as the soul of the home. Breaking bread has traditionally been considered a quintessential gesture of hospitality, and the dining room was the inevitable setting for every occasion involving guests and food. As most bungalow households did not include servants, visitors were further honored by the housewife's culinary skills. It was hoped that the room's decoration and the display of various dining-room furnishings would also make a good impression.

For most, thoughts of the dining room are usually evoked with fondness. Many people share their earliest memories of a big table bedecked with party favors and a birthday cake and ringed by dressed-up children. More routinely, the dining room's location was poised within earshot of mother in the kitchen or father in the living room, which made it a good place for doing homework. Other memorable moments might include festive holiday gatherings, with the entire family joined by close relatives gathered around the table.

The practical use of the bungalow's dining room parallels that of its Victorian predecessor. Throughout the nineteenth century, the American dining room had become increasingly important as a setting for family life. This importance is emphasized by the fact that many Victorian dining rooms are significantly larger than the parlor. One of the key places for household members to gather, it was where the taste and social standing of the family could also be displayed to guests. Offering a particularly appropriate setting to showcase the family's "good" furniture, china,

crystal, silver, and linens, it became the room that most expressed the homeowner's values.

Even by the turn of the century, as the bungalow was emerging as a new housing form, the public was still not ready to relinquish in the name of convenience or practicality everything familiar and held dear about earlier houses. While some house plans combined living and dining functions into a single multipurpose room, it is more usual for even very modest bungalows to have a separate dining room.

Its central position in most floor plans places the dining room next to the living room. Where floor space was at a premium, creating a feeling of roominess was a high design priority. The popular colonnade arrangement of partial walls or built-ins surmounted by short columns was much used for this purpose (figs. 68, 76). Some dining rooms had useful built-in china cabinets that were placed back-to-back with shelving in the living room. Equally important with the sense of spaciousness shared by the two rooms was the feeling of privacy made possible by having pocket doors that could close between the living and dining rooms. Pocket doors were sometimes fitted with clear or leaded art-glass panels. Because of their lower cost, simpler mechanism, and open and airy effect, French doors became increasingly popular for use between rooms by the Twenties. Not as space-efficient, their door swings tended to inhibit furniture arrangement in small houses, and many have since been removed.

The popularity of portières was a distinct carry-over from the Victorian era. Even when closed off by pocket doors, wide doorways could also be softened with the addition of these full-height draperies, which were an effective way to incorporate textiles into the decoration schemes of homes. They also cut down on drafts, muffled noise, and even helped to conserve heat in the winter. Sometimes a

64. Dining room scheme. Showcasing some of the offerings in their extensive line, this was an illustration in the 1914–1915 catalog of James Davis Artistic Paperhangings of Chicago. It highlights a wide frieze depicting a panoramic mountain landscape, which provides considerable dramatic impact for the room. Making possible exceptionally refined detail and blended color effects intended to resemble those of hand painting, this particular frieze was lithographed and imported from Germany. It was far more usual and much less expensive for wallpapers to be conventionally roller-printed by machine, as most had been since the mid-nineteenth century. Sold in a series of separate side-matched panels, this design could form a mural on a single wall, or run continuously around the room, as seen here. Placed between the typical box-beam ceiling and high wainscot, the frieze boldly plays on the idea of bringing nature indoors. Topped by a wooden plate rail, the unusual design of the wainscot is created by collaging paper border and background elements together, and their arrangement was inspired by the vertical wood battens and panels of conventional wainscots. Marketed at the time as an alternative to more costly woodwork and painted effects, the wallpaper's mottled background texture, combined with its rich color accents, convincingly replicates the look of handpainted wall finishes and stenciling. Showing the influence of the Colonial Revival style, the furniture is loosely adapted from the seventeenth-century English Jacobean style, characterized by the turned legs. Dining sets similar to what is shown here became very popular in the Twenties, and free-standing sideboards gradually supplanted the built-ins. The room's elaborate walls are offset by a plain, room-size carpet with a solid green border, the color of which coordinates with the upholstery of the dining chairs.

different fabric or color was used on either side of the portière to coordinate with the scheme of the room it faced. Most were hung on simple metal or wooden rods from exposed rings. A favorite device of the Arts and Crafts style, portières were often made more splendid with hand embroidery, appliqué designs, or stenciling. Table linens were also important to the household at that time, and embroidery kits for tablecloths and matching napkins were widely available (fig. 68). When the dining table was not set for a meal, table runners or scarves were often used to dress its surface (figs. 64, 65, 66, 71, 72, 76), and could even be coordinated with the curtains (fig. 69) or other decoration (fig. 66). As in some living rooms, dining rooms might also have a built-in windowseat, so there was an opportunity to introduce or repeat a fabric in the cushions or some handwork on decorated pillows (fig. 68).

While it was not unheard of for a bungalow dining room to have a fireplace (fig. 9), it was more usual to be able to see the living-room fireplace from the dining room (fig. 68). In the Craftsman taste, one of the most frequently incorporated millwork details in bungalow dining rooms is a high wainscot topped by a plate rail (or shallow, grooved shelf). Sometimes this treatment also finds its way into living and other rooms. Another common feature, the use of box beams to divide the ceiling into panels, continues the Craftsman emphasis on structural forms for design interest (figs. 64, 66, 76). Encouraged by Gustav Stickley's advice, some people did experiment with adding color, such as green or silvery gray, to their woodwork, usually in the living and dining rooms, where it would be most likely to be seen by guests. Some examples of this use of color still exist.

Dining-room floors were generally of the same material and design as those in the living room. Hardwood floors were usually stained to darken them slightly before they were varnished. However, most bungalow hardwood floors are decidedly lighter in value than the other unpainted woodwork in the room. Wood floors were most often covered with a room-size area rug, which was always centered under the dining table. It was fairly common for hardwood floors to be inlaid with contrasting strips of a darker-stained, or even a different type of wood (fig. 75). Such inlaid effects would often include ornamental detailing, such as a geometric knot or similar flourish at each corner. Gustav Stickley promoted the idea of using wood floors with inlaid decorative borders inspired by Native American designs, and also was receptive to using wood other than oak, such as maple or even some tropical hardwoods, for their variations in color. Hand-woven Oriental carpets, or machine-made copies, probably enjoyed the greatest popularity (figs. 70, 73, 75). Some rug designs reflected simpler, more abstract geometric designs (fig. 74), and possibly even a Native American influence. Other less expensive types of rugs might even be made of natural materials or matting, such as sisal or jute, which for some offered enough beauty as a natural material. Gustav Stickley also designed and marketed such rugs under the Craftsman banner, which included examples made of wool and jute. Also popular was the simplicity of solid-color rugs, some of which were given interest by the use of a border in a solid contrasting color (figs. 64, 65).

Of all of the built-ins in the house, few were more important than the dining-room sideboard. A focal point, similar to the role of the fireplace in the living room, it symbolized much about the quality and comfort of home life. Many dining rooms were arranged so that their sideboard was opposite the doorway into the living room (figs. 67, 70, 76). Frequently called a buffet in plan books, sideboards epitomized the convenience of built-ins, as they were among the most practical of any in the house. Their popularity can be traced to their medieval origins, when they developed in aristocratic households as places to display the family's wealth to visitors, which was sometimes literally represented by a rich array of gold and silver vessels or serving pieces. Not originating as a built-in, their utility for food service also evolved later, but their association with display, geared for guests, survives to this day. Bungalow sideboards were potentially one of the bulkiest of all built-ins and needed to be carefully designed or chosen to complement but not overwhelm the room.

Most sideboards found in bungalows reflect the simpler lines and detailing of the Craftsman style (fig. 74). With classically inspired columns or moldings, some combine traces of the Colonial Revival style (figs. 65, 75). Others may have more severe lines and geometric art-glass designs influenced by the Midwest Prairie style (figs. 70, 71, 73, 74). Dining rooms of Mission or Spanish Colonial Revival style bungalows are less likely to have a built-in sideboard, or as many other built-ins, as the other bungalow styles.

Unless opting for a custom-designed unit, most people scoured home magazines, plan books, and millwork catalogs for sideboard ideas. To conserve open floor space, most bungalow floor plans allowed the sideboard to be recessed into the wall. It was also common for some to be placed on a window wall (figs. 71, 74), or contained entirely within a bay window. China storage was accommodated in the upper cabinets, for its visibility was preferred. There were many choices of glass-fronted door styles available, including plain or divided lights, just beveled, variations of leaded (figs. 70, 74, 76), leaded and beveled, or leaded and stained art glass (figs. 67, 68, 71, 73). A generously wide serving-height surface was a must, and to reflect light and better display ornamental glass or serving pieces, the back panel behind it was usually mirrored (figs. 66, 70, 74, 76). If set into a wall abutting the kitchen, a sliding pass-through door was frequently fitted into the back panel (a convenience also seen in some Victorian sideboards). Drawers for silverware and table linens and cupboards for storing large serving pieces were standard equipment for most sideboards.

Dining rooms generally had a central ceiling fixture, and the available styles varied enormously. Largely a matter of personal taste and budget, probably the least expensive fixtures were the suspended glass-bowl type (fig. 67). Different versions were commonly used in every bungalow room, except the kitchen. Gustav Stickley recommended the use of single lights, suspended from individual chains, to be arranged in a line above the length of the dining room table (fig. 66). Single lights were also commonly suspended from or surface-mounted on intersections of box beams (fig. 66). Assemblies of multiple single fixtures, suspended from a common backplate, were described as the "shower" type. Formed of square brass tubing, there was a prevalence of simply detailed, multiarm fixtures (figs. 70, 73, 74), some with art-glass shades (figs. 68, 69, 72). Wall-mounted lights and sconces (with arms and back plates) were also popular, especially with a matching ceiling fixture (figs. 70, 72). Occasionally, wall lights were directly attached to the framework of the sideboard (figs. 70, 76); sideboards also might be fitted with smaller lights on the underside of their china cabinets (fig. 66). The better to illuminate the table, but to avoid glare, low-hanging fixtures were a solution. Simple forms, such as pyramidal shapes (figs. 75, 76) in metal and stained glass were popular and affordable choices. Some fixtures featured glass-beaded fringe around their bottoms as a decorative way to help shield the light.

It was fundamentally important that the dining room directly adjoin the kitchen (figs. 67, 70, 71, 73) even if by way of a walk-through pantry, which was less common. A two-way swinging door was a useful feature found in virtually every bungalow. As with their living rooms, it was desirable to have direct access to a porch or garden area (figs. 67, 70, 72, 74, 75). Besides their doors to the kitchen and living room, dining rooms frequently had single doorways opening into short hallways, which led to the bathroom and bedrooms (fig. 76).

With such a preponderance of door openings and a minimum of wall space, it was helpful that so much of a bungalow's dining-room furniture was either built in, or placed at its center. Nevertheless, some of the most coveted of all Arts and Crafts-style furniture was created for dining room use, particularly sideboards or servers (figs. 66, 71, 74), which sometimes eclipsed the style and craftsmanship, if not the utility, of the typical built-in example.

65. Breakfast room scheme. Some bungalows had separate breakfast rooms, which was a more gracious alternative to the minimal scale of the breakfast nook located within the kitchen. If a family's space requirements were particularly tight, a room like this could also serve as a den, sewing room, or even a small bedroom. In this rendering from a linoleum advertisement, the manufacturer wanted to show how one of their tile-like flooring patterns, if extended from a kitchen into an adjoining room, could expand the feeling of space. The Colonial Revival style of the Twenties is seen in the white-painted woodwork, classically detailed corner cupboard, and dining furniture, adapted from eighteenth and early nineteenth-century American designs. Visible through the doorway, a wide porcelain-enameled cast-iron kitchen sink with legs has an integral backsplash. The diamond-paned casement window above the sink is certainly not typical of bungalow kitchens. The window at the left of the table has a painted wooden valance, brightly patterned curtains, and glass shelves to show off colorful objects in the sunshine.

66. Dining room of a Windsor Square District house, Los Angeles, California. In this 1912 house, a significant collection of Arts and Crafts furniture and objects is displayed against a period background. In this dining room, the owners, film director Scott Goldstein and his wife, set decorator and designer Lauren Gabor, have skillfully enhanced existing original features by using appropriate color, pattern, and textiles. At the center of a shallow box beam on the ceiling and placed lengthwise above the table, are five suspended lights with Steuben-glass shades in a group design recommended by Gustav Stickley. Another decorative device favored by Stickley is the crossed table scarves, which are hand-embroidered with one of his designs. Surmounted at its center by a china cabinet is an original built-in sideboard with a long serving surface that extends below a pair of windows, and which has a light reflected in the mirrored panel. Crowning the room is a handsome stenciled frieze, adapted by Goldstein from a period design. The Gustav Stickley "V-back" chairs retain their original leather upholstery. On the table are settings of Arts and Crafts period silverware and a rare set of Revere Pottery/Saturday Evening Girls dishes that are laid out for an afternoon tea. At right, a copper and mica lamp by Dirk Van Erp, a leading metalsmith of the period, glows softly on a small Gustav Stickley sideboard from 1901. (For other views of this house see figs. 169–172 in *The Bungalow.*)

(*Overleaf*) 67. Dining room in Long Beach, California. A group of distinctively designed French doors framed in narrow panels inset with colored glass admits golden light to the dining room, and allows access to a raised terrace on the side of this 1913 bungalow. The fir woodwork detailing throughout these rooms employs a series of small squared corbels supporting the plate rail of the wainscot and overhangs above the doorways and sideboard. The dining room's focal point, when viewed from the living room, is a handsome sideboard on the far wall centered between two doors. Flanked by full-height tapering pilasters, the three-part cabinet sideboard is topped by an original sloping mirrored panel, which enables those seated at the table to see their reflections. Geometric leaded art-glass panels in the cabinet doors repeat the colored glass in the French doors. In the far corner a swinging door opens into a breakfast room with light-painted woodwork, which features a high wainscot and a smaller sideboard also with leaded-glass cabinets. A room-wide doorway is framed by a large overhead beam and a pair of low walls that terminate in massive, square, newel-like posts, which make good display pedestals for pottery. (For another view of this house see fig. 15.)

68. Dining room in Los Angeles, California. The characteristic bungalow colonnade effect, created by a partial-height screen wall supporting a pair of squared columns, allows long views between the dining and living rooms. Replicating their original painted finish, the deep color of the walls complements the complex figuring in the grain of the stained-fir woodwork. The current owners put a major effort into stripping and refinishing the woodwork, which was painted white when they purchased the West Adams district bungalow. A recessed window at right has a built-in seat, which runs almost the full length of the room. A pillow features a period textile design adapted from one by Gustav Stickley, and on the round table is an embroidered textile from the period. (For another view of this house see fig. 42.)

69. Dining area in Marin County, California. Renovated in period style by its current owner, the house forms a sensitively designed setting for a comprehensive collection of Arts and Crafts furniture, paintings, and objects. Throughout the house, there are period lighting fixtures of exceptional quality. Above the table, a four-arm brass light fixture has squared lines and tapering square art-glass shades in a geometric pattern. Visible in the living area beyond is an unusual ceiling-mounted Handel fixture with a triangulated back-plate and four hanging glass shades. The oak fireplace mantel is of the period and was added in the recent renovation along with an appropriate tile surround. An imposing Handel floor lamp stands next to a substantial Arts and Crafts settle, the architectural lines of which make it an effective room divider. The wall and ceiling finish, a softly sponge-painted golden hue, is amplified by the area's abundant natural light. The elegant period design of the carpet, custom made for this space, suits the lines of the dining table and chairs. The table, a rare and custom-made Gustav Stickley piece, is overlaid with a long table runner that coordinates with the curtains. On it are a Rookwood vase, and a pair of gracefully attenuated Tiffany candlesticks. (For other views of this house see illustration facing page 1 and figs. 89, 110, 120, 121.)

70. Dining room in South Pasadena, California. On a far wall, between a pair of doors, is this dining room's particularly wide sideboard. In the Craftsman taste, a pair of original wall lights are mounted directly on fir casings on either side of the sideboard. Stretched out above the serving surface of the sideboard, two pairs of leaded-glass cabinet doors feature stylized tulip designs, and in the far right corner, the same motif is repeated in the leaded window of the swinging door to the kitchen. Backlit by a long mirrored panel, a collection of Roseville pottery is displayed on the sideboard. The dining-room furniture is recreated from Stickley designs. The room's ceiling and upper walls merge in one continuous sweep to make a coved ceiling, which was popular in the early twentieth century, carried over from the late nineteenth century. The house dates from 1914.

71. Raised open dining area, Berkeley, California. From its elevated position on a raised platform there is a good view of the entire living area. Within view of seated diners is a fireplace centered in an alcove at the left. Visible is one of two deeply cushioned built-in seats next to the fireplace. An elegantly understated, built-in sideboard on the far wall has a geometric art-glass design in its glass china-cabinet doors reminiscent of the Prairie style. Accents of period-style textile designs provide a soft counterpoint to the wealth of rustic wood. In the far corner, an open door leads to a light-filled kitchen. Even with such an eclectic mix of furniture styles, the strength of the architecture makes a definitive Craftsman-style statement. (For other views of this house see figs. 17, 43.)

72. Dining room in Seattle, Washington. The wide doorway at right reveals the fireplace in the living room. At left is a pair of French doors with leaded grids that suggest an abstract tree design. The 1909 house was completely renovated to designs by the Johnson Partnership, a Seattle architectural firm sympathetic to old houses. All in English Arts and Crafts style, the oak dining furniture includes the distinctive flat-topped china cabinet standing to the left of the wide doorway into the living room. Some plates recreated in Pre-Raphaelite style sit on the plate rail at the right of the wide doorway. The elegantly styled brass and stained-glass ceiling period fixture matches a pair of wall lights that are visible above the fireplace mantel. (For another view of this house see fig. 51.)

73. Dining room in San Diego, California. When the current owners first saw this room, it had been stripped of virtually every vestige of its original character; a victim of the familiar scenario of modernization. Despite its defilement, this bungalow still managed to charm them into saving it, and with the help of restoration consultant Jim Gibson, they have made great strides in recreating its appropriate period atmosphere. Guided by the "ghost" lines that were left by previously removed elements, a built-in sideboard, wainscoting, and various wide moldings were put back. With the freedom of having nothing existing to match, their decision to combine and contrast light-colored birch with darker redwood has produced a lively varied effect. Wanting to admit as much light as possible, the owners installed a generous amount of newly crafted art glass in a pair of windows and French doors leading to an enclosed sunporch. The stylized tree design in the glass was inspired by Frank Lloyd Wright's Prairie-style work. The china cabinet doors have matching art glass. The dining table and chairs, chosen for their contrast with the surrounding woodwork, are recreated Gustav Stickley designs in dark stained oak. The house was built in 1913 in an enclave of curving streets and pink concrete sidewalks called the Burlingame development. East of Balboa Park and on the edge of a rustic canyon, it adjoins the larger North Park neighborhood. The range of diverse and largely intact architecture of this area has inspired many of its residents to become active in promoting community awareness, staging house tours, and encouraging preservation.

74. Dining room in Pasadena, California. The striking and unusual built-in sideboard at the far end of this room reveals the inventive hand of its architect, Frederick Louis Roehrig. The lower doors and cupboards are arranged almost as if to create the space for a chair. A pair of tall china cabinets at left and right with leaded-glass doors creates a recess for the windows. Gustav Stickley furniture includes the set of "H-back" chairs, the square table with its angled base design, and the freestanding sideboard at right. The plate rail, where objects are again displayed, had been removed; using family photographs obtained from former owners, it has since been replaced. The distinctively divided windows are used throughout the house, as seen in the casement at the right. A horizontal cross bar is placed near the top and bottom of each window sash. Commended during the Craftsman era for its unpretentious, natural texture, the horizontal flow of the grasscloth echoes the lines of the room and adds a warm subtle color to its walls. The house was built in 1908 in the Oak Knoll area.

(Overleaf) 75. Dining room in Oakland, California. In a skillful remodeling of this warmly inviting room by local architect Glen Jarvis of Jarvis Architects, an outside door to a new deck was added in the far corner. When closed, the door effectively masquerades as another window, for its proportion and detailing duplicate that of the casement window it replaced. At the right is a linen Roman shade that the owners stenciled with an Arts and Crafts floral motif. They also made the two matching pillows on the settee. The sturdy armchairs are recycled vintage office furniture. In the recess below a pair of horizontal casement windows at the left the built-in shelves display a collection of pottery. The Douglas fir ceiling beams are structural floor joists, instead of being strictly decorative box beams. The high wainscot and other millwork detailing of this room matches that of the living room. A plate rail, supported by a bold dentil molding, holds a large collection of basketwork that provides an important element of texture and design to the room. (For other views of this house see figs. 22, 28, 90.)

76. Dining room in Los Angeles, California. Exhibiting some rather original ideas, the furnishings of this dining room show the ingenuity of its owner, who got a lot of impact out of a limited budget. This novel solution for accommodating guests in a Craftsman-style room grew out of a clever idea. A large slab of clear beveled glass was placed on top of a small Craftsman library table, thus creating of much larger table to sit eight. Visits to swap meets yielded eight almost matching examples of vintage wooden library chairs. It was as much for their pleasing form and durability as for their price or their slatted backs that they were purchased. In a color similar to the matte-green glazes of the pottery collection on the sideboard tie-on cushions cover the seats. For over fifteen years the owner has searched for pieces in this color range, assembling a number from Roseville's "Egypto" series, and from other noted potteries like Teco, Grueby, and Hampshire. The elegant built-in sideboard is framed with tall, tapering pilasters that are mounted with light fixtures. Next to the pilasters, two of the four leaded-glass cabinet doors are installed at a slight angle to create further design interest. At the right, a Roycroft oval copper tray is displayed on a small oak server by Limbert. Because it was completely covered with white paint when the house was purchased, returning the fir wood-work to its original state has made everything else about restoring this bungalow seem easy. Once stripped, it was given a mahogany-color stain before varnishing. As a finishing touch, the owner opted to use an appropriate Arts and Crafts wallpaper and border above the wain-scot. Although the papers chosen are hand-printed, the relatively small quantity required for this room made their purchase very reasonable. In a final flourish, the owner chose to paint the ceiling panels between the box beams a lustrous metallic gold, which creates richly reflective effects especially at night. Similar metallic ceiling finishes were actually employed in the period. Sometimes achieved with paint only, a metallic gold, bronze, or copper-color finish might also be applied to a textured fabric like burlap, or even to embossed wallcoverings.

The Kitchen
REALM OF DOMESTICITY

While warm firesides and hospitable settings were important, the greatest innovations in housing at the turn of the century were the technological advances in the middle-class kitchen. Since the bungalow market was largely made up of the younger generation, its prospective homemakers were more likely to be receptive to new ways of doing things around the kitchen than their parents might have been. Because of this, the marketing of the bungalow was accordingly pursued with a double effectiveness. On one hand, it aimed to appeal to the public's sense of traditional comforts and values; on the other, it also answered their increasing demands for more modern conveniences and gadgetry.

Kitchens are probably the most indispensable room in any house because to live, we all must eat. In order to do so at home, we all need a place to prepare our food. Once this basic need has been met, finding a place to eat is always an easier proposition. Likewise, almost all other functions of daily domestic life can be performed in settings different from those that were designed for them. The kitchen, however, a self-contained world, has a distinct set of rules and sense of place. There are many that would name it as their favorite room in the house.

The place around which so much of family life revolves, kitchens are inevitably caught up in much household lore and memories. Closely tied to our most basic feelings of security and well being, the kitchen can remind us to count our blessings and appreciate the basic comfort of knowing that there will be food for our next meal. This was the setting where many of life's basic lessons were indelibly imparted to children. Most of us learned about basic economy and the importance of not wasting valuable resources through parallel experiences concerning food. The importance of safety issues, whether concerning heat, fire, use of appliances, cooking implements, or even toxic substances,

were probably first coached in the kitchen setting. There were also the lessons of care and maintenance, from dishes and pot-scrubbing to polishing silver or helping with the laundry.

Our sense of smell is said to be the most powerful of all in terms of recollection, and the kitchen was seldom without aromas. While everyone has their own personal favorites, each time of day and each meal brought a different aroma rising from the stove or wafting through the house. Taste impressions also tend to linger, and it seemed in childhood that there could never be enough really good ones. The transforming powers of the oven's heat was one of the earliest "miracles" a child's eye was likely to observe. This was also the room where young children would gain personal confidence by following their first recipe and having its results well received.

It was the housewife who ruled the kitchen not only in cooking but also in matters concerning purchasing and storing food and supplies. Women were the driving force behind evolving kitchen technology because they were the ones who would be liberated by it. In terms of making the kitchen a pleasanter environment, the housewife was the primary motivating factor.

Kitchens were traditionally considered utility areas, and many floorplans included small utility porches, often fitted with a deep laundry sink, which had other household uses in addition to cradling the washboard. In the earlier examples the refrigerators that required ice, thus usually called iceboxes, were generally located as close to the back door as possible to facilitate deliveries of ice (fig. 77). Milkmen were sometimes able to make deliveries or retrieve empty bottles through a convenient covered compartment with a lift-up door. Handy during inclement weather, this also allowed access from inside the house.

Electricity for domestic use was well established by the

77. Scheme for a kitchen. With its sunny atmosphere and steaming teakettle, this picture evokes an ideal bungalow kitchen. The illustration was used in a promotional book called *Floors, Furniture and Color* published in 1924 by the Linoleum Division of the Armstrong Cork Company of Lancaster, Pennsylvania, to promote linoleum flooring like the blue and gray tile pattern seen here. The inviting breakfast nook, portrayed here as a roomy area, was usually much more confined. Built-in tables like the one shown were often hinged on the inside wall to swing up for easier seating or for more convenient cleaning. The curved arms of the high-back benches is a Colonial Revival touch. Although this kitchen's walls, woodwork, and built-ins are painted white, the color in the windows, curtains, and stool indicate the increasing trend to make kitchens more pleasant. A white-painted icebox built under a small window is partly visible on the utility porch. The gas range is raised on curving metal legs and is characteristic of many stoves of the Twenties. Such stoves were available in bright enamel finishes, including white, cream, and pale green.

78. Hoosier cabinet. A veritable microcosm of bungalow planning philosophy, this space- and step-saving cabinet appears to place almost every cooking utensil and material close at hand. It could also expand available work space with its pull-out worksurface. This is only one of many models of similar freestanding kitchen cabinets for which the Hoosier Manufacturing Company of New Castle, Indiana, became famous. This illustration appeared in *Home Interiors*, a design-advice book published in 1917 by *Good Furniture Magazine* of Grand Rapids, Michigan. At upper left, a flour bin has a built-in sifter. In addition to the handy extra drawer space, family dishes could be housed in the upper cupboard. Although floor space was at a premium in most bungalow kitchens, there was probably a Hoosier cabinet model that could be fit in somewhere. Although this example shows its original natural wood finish, many were painted to match their neighboring built-ins.

end of the nineteenth century, yet it continued to be considered an option for some households. Depending on the location or the capability of the local utility, it was not uncommon for bungalows to be outfitted for both gas and electrical service. By the Twenties, electricity became standard in most homes, and electric refrigerators replaced iceboxes (fig. 80). Many bungalows featured food-storage cabinets that were naturally cooled by fresh air drawn in from the outside or from underneath the house through screen-covered openings (fig. 82). Popularly known as coolers (or California coolers) these conveniences persisted in many homes long after electric refrigeration became commonplace, for their ability to hold a steady temperature still suited some types of food storage. Even if coolers have been blocked off, they remain useful space for other storage.

Electricity became important in many bungalow kitchens for running the tabletop appliances and gadgetry that were flooding the consumer market (fig. 79). Fed by popular advertising, the push was to shun the old fashioned and pursue the modern. To its advantage, the bungalow was caught in the middle, and it became known as the most modern and up-to-date home. Probably the most popular convenience item in almost every bungalow was the folding ironing board with its cubbyhole for storing the electric iron. In addition to electric fans there were many other countertop favorites: toasters, teakettles, coffee pots, waffle irons, frying pans, and chafing dishes, which were widely promoted as timesavers for entertaining. Already in use were pioneering examples of the electric laundry machine, and early versions of the electric dishwasher appeared in the Twenties.

Despite its rapid rise in popularity, electricity certainly couldn't replace every use of natural gas, for there were ways in which it continued to excel in performance and economy. A major innovation in stoves occurred when they were powered entirely by gas (figs. 77, 80) rather than fueled by coal or wood, as most were during the nineteenth century. Cleanliness, convenience, and more easily controlled heating levels were the big advantages of gas. Gas-powered water heaters, which were often referred to as boilers, became staples of the bungalow kitchen, or perhaps its back porch. The narrow diameter of the earlier models sometimes enabled them to be built in and vented near the stove, behind a cabinet door (fig. 80). The use of gas to power furnaces for heat was also developing at this time, and gas stoves and gas heat persist to this day. Electric stoves were slower to be perfected, and didn't come into common use until some years after the bungalow's decline.

Separate from its other attractions, the bungalow would gain renown and popularity for its concerted effort to improve the life of the housewife. A simple step in this direction was to accommodate a place for eating within the confines of the kitchen. The breakfast nook (sometimes also called a dining nook or breakfast alcove) was the compact eating area that sprouted up in many bungalows, particularly in houses of the later Teens and Twenties (fig. 77). Extremely popular, they appear in many of the floorplans published in periodicals and plan books (fig. 11). Most nooks have a narrow rectangular table set between a facing pair of built-in benches. Designed to fit into almost impossibly tight spaces, some models featured a lift-up, folding, or sliding tabletop to make it easier to get in or out (fig. 85). Millwork catalogs illustrated breakfast nooks that could be purchased as complete, ready-to-install units.

Predictably, such catalogs did an especially brisk business in the sales of kitchen cabinets of all sizes and types. It was not unusual for a bungalow kitchen wall to have floor-to-ceiling cabinets (fig. 86). The familiar upper and lower cabinet arrangement was more common to maximize the available worksurface. Sinks were usually placed on an outside wall beneath windows for light and views of the garden or playing children (fig. 77). Most sinks were single-basin, porcelain-finished cast-iron, and some had a high backsplash as part of the unit. These could either be set into the surrounding countertop surface or mounted independently on the wall (fig. 77). There were also other types of sink available with integral drainboards, a very practical innovation (fig. 82). Some sink units were comfortably wide and set on tall metal or matching porcelain-finish legs. Cabinet styles were invariably quite simple, usually with a single flat recessed panel and strictly functional hardware. Some cabinets had glass-fronted doors usually in their upper portion, so that the contents of the cabinet could easily be seen. Many bungalows incorporated useful deep pull-out bins and slide-out cutting boards that doubled as expandable worksurfaces (fig. 82). The majority of kitchen cabinets were made of fir and were intended to be painted. However, a number of existing examples and early photographs prove that some people did prefer their kitchen cabinets to retain their natural wood finish along with the rest of the home's woodwork. For many American kitchens the free-standing and multipurpose fixture, called a Hoosier cabinet (after the name of the manufacturer) became very popular (fig. 78). Its abundance of specially sized storage areas, pull-out bins, flour sifter, and various nooks and crannies for small and indispensable kitchen items, is legendary. It was a godsend for many small bungalow kitchens that were otherwise short on space.

In the early twentieth century, most kitchens were still purely utilitarian with little concession to ornamental effects. White continued to predominate on walls, woodwork, and cabinets, being preferred for its continuing association with sanitation and usually achieved with durable enamel paint. The use of more color began slowly to appear in bungalow kitchens (fig. 77). Usually made in designs that resembled ceramic tile, there were specialty wallcoverings called sanitary papers (or just sanitaries) that were varnished after installation for greater washability. Another treatment for the lower portion of kitchen or bathroom walls was to score and paint the plaster to mimic tile. In homes with bigger budgets, ceramic tile was often preferred for its tidy look and easily cleaned surface (fig. 173).

Countertops were often surfaced with small white porcelain hexagonal tiles with a matte finish (fig. 81), which were sometimes also used for kitchen flooring (fig. 82). Sometimes these floors were enlivened by colored tiles that were placed to create a simple overall pattern. Sometimes plain white tile countertops were trimmed in glazed tiles of a contrasting color and eventually there were similar tile borders for backsplashes (fig. 81). If more than one countertop surface existed in the same kitchen, wood was likely to be one of them (fig. 82).

Bungalow kitchen floors were most commonly made of fir (fig. 88). If the budget allowed, many people preferred the greater durability of a hardwood floor (figs. 85, 86, 88, 89, 90), and the tight grain of maple was a good alternate

to the usual oak (fig. 173). The use of small throw rugs was common in kitchens, which helped to preserve the flooring, and also added some color and design interest (fig. 88). Many wood floors were overlaid with a patterned linoleum. Extremely durable and easy to maintain, tile-like designs were most popular for kitchens and frequently covered the entire floor area (fig. 77), an effect that has been commonly replicated in vinyl flooring (figs. 80, 83). Room-size linoleum "rugs" were also available. They allowed a portion of the wood floors to show, and their popularity persisted for many years. Available in a remarkable variety of designs that approximated everything from ceramic tile to Oriental carpets, linoleum could be used in every room of the house (figs. 56, 78).

Significant use of color was more likely to occur in bungalow kitchens of the late Twenties. Color could always be inexpensively added by cheerfully patterned curtains or painted accents on the window sash, cabinets, or other built-ins (fig. 77). Because of their constant use kitchens were especially subject to remodeling or upgrading within a decade or two after they had been built (fig. 81). The continuous innovations in the bungalow kitchen helped to facilitate its gradual image makeover from a bland utility area into a vibrant center of family living.

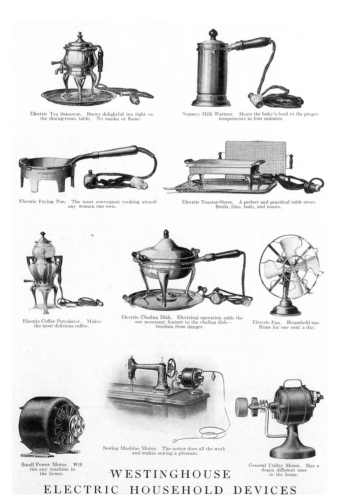

Electric Tea Samovar. Brews delightful tea right on the dining-room table. No smoke or flame.

Nursery Milk Warmer. Heats the baby's food to the proper temperature in four minutes.

Electric Frying Pan. The most convenient cooking utensil any woman can own.

Electric Toaster-Stove. A perfect and practical table stove. Broils, fries, boils, and toasts.

Electric Coffee Percolator. Makes the most delicious coffee.

Electric Chafing Dish. Electrical operation adds the one necessary feature to the chafing dish—freedom from danger.

Electric Fan. Household size. Runs for one cent a day.

Sewing Machine Motor. The motor does all the work and makes sewing a pleasure.

Small Power Motor. Will run any machine in the house.

General Utility Motor. Has a dozen different uses in the home.

WESTINGHOUSE
ELECTRIC HOUSEHOLD DEVICES

79. Electric household devices. These are just a few examples of the new electric gadgetry that flooded the market during the rise of the bungalow. Illustrated in a 1917 book about current design trends called *Home Interiors* these items were "hot" household news and regarded as indispensable equipment for the truly modern home. Examples include (from left to right, and top to bottom): an electric tea samovar, a nursery milk warmer, a frying pan, a "toaster-stove," a coffee percolator, a chafing dish, a fan, a small power motor (that "will run any machine in the house"), a sewing machine, and a general utility motor (claiming to have "a dozen different uses in the house"). These particular examples were manufactured by Westinghouse, who had plenty of competition in the burgeoning home-appliances market of the early twentieth century.

80. Gas stove and electric refrigerator. Jauntily perched on curving metal legs, these vintage appliances are in good working order, and their future is secure in this kitchen of a 1919 bungalow located in the North Park neighborhood of San Diego. The perfectly functioning 36"-wide stove was purchased by the homeowner from a local used-appliance dealer, who specializes in refurbishing such early examples. It bears the shield-shaped Barker Brothers crest, the name of a Southern California furniture-store chain that was prominent during the bungalow era. Dating from the mid-twenties, ranges similar to this example were scaled to fit compact bungalow kitchens. Its popular white porcelain finish with black trim was an industry standard, although other more decorative color combinations, incorporating white, black, or cream with blue or green, were also available from most manufacturers. Built in 1933, the "Monitor top" refrigerator features the distinctive top-mounted circular cooling coils, and it was manufactured by General Electric. Perfect for bungalows, this was the smallest model made and measures only about 24" square. Because it is top-heavy and awkward to move, it now stands on industrial casters to enable easier cleaning and maintenance. The vinyl-tile flooring recreates a popular vintage linoleum pattern from the Twenties. (For another view of this house see fig. 43 in *The Bungalow*.)

81. Kitchen in the Randall house, Berkeley, California. Almost as it was when the house was constructed for local civil engineer Henry I. Randall in 1909, this kitchen shows how it continues to be convenient and serviceable. This view shows a characteristic placement of the sink below a pair of small windows. An original light fixture is on the wall between them. Possibly added in the Twenties, the sink's countertop incorporates a pair of drainboards surfaced with small white hexagonal tiles trimmed with black. The backsplash is made with yellow tiles accented by a narrow black-and-white ceramic border. Tall built-in upper cabinets flank the sink area, with drawer and cupboard units below. A vintage toaster is on a small counter area near the corner, and below it there is a pull-out bin next to a unit with drawers. The period overhead light fixture would have been more typical in a bungalow dining room than in a kitchen. A perennially popular Twenties linoleum pattern, recreated in sheet vinyl, makes a practical flooring surface with a period feeling. (For other views of this house see figs. 150–153 in *The Bungalow*.)

82. Butler's pantry in the Lanterman House (El Retiro), La Canada Flintridge, California. Although it is part of an extraordinary and over-sized 1915 Craftsman-style bungalow, this butler's pantry is included here because it so closely resembles the scale and features of the kitchens in more modest bungalows. Rarely preserved just as they originated, such kitchens are less likely to survive than bathrooms. At the left, upper and lower cabinet doors are open to a large, two-tier California cooler, a food storage innovation of the day. To maintain an even temperature, it was designed to draw fresh outside air through screened openings. This example takes air from both above and below the house, although most units were vented directly through an outside wall. Another staple of bungalow-kitchen cabinetry that was popular in the late Victorian era is the opened bin. The white, matte-finish hexagonal ceramic tile floor has a module size that is somewhat larger than usual. More expensive than linoleum, it was commonly used for bathroom floors, and forms an extremely practical, low-maintenance sur-face. Wall-mounted, but also supported by the cabinets beneath, the wide cast-iron sink has a high backsplash and pair of generous drain-boards. Also original to the house, a smattering of vintage kitchen bowls, utensils, and early electric appliances are displayed on the countertops. (For other views of this house see figs. 128–131 in *The Bungalow*.)

83. Kitchen in Spokane, Washington. When the current owners bought it, the kitchen of this early Twenties bungalow in the South Hill area had been drastically altered. Inspired by the intact Craftsman-style exterior of the house, they decided to create a kitchen design that would be sympathetic and appropriate for their home. Factors of personal style and budget guided their decision against slavishly replicating what might have originally been there. To claim as much open space as possible they decided to absorb a small breakfast room previously located at the far end of this space. They also eliminated a second door into the dining room, thus gaining needed wall space in both rooms. By stripping the window sashes, they restored the appealing period design of the original double-hung windows, which became a new focal point in the kitchen. Additional smaller windows were added above the counter at left. To retain the maximum effect of open space the use of upper cabinets was avoided, although some were used above the refrigerator at right. Some open shelving was also installed at the opposite end of the room (fig. 84). The ready-made cabinets, in a natural wood finish, were selected for their simple recessed panels, similar to what was seen in many original bungalow kitchens. Uniting the far corners of the room, a high continuous display shelf forms an ideal stage for a collection of vintage ceramic refrigerator jugs.

84. Open kitchen shelving in Spokane, Washington. As an alternative to kitchen cabinets with doors, the use of open shelving, especially for storing frequently used items, can be an effective solution, for it can help create extra space. In this example, the wood shelves are painted a soft green to harmonize with other elements in this kitchen (fig. 83). The shelves are supported by sturdy wooden brackets. These are mounted against a wall that is faced with beadboard, sometimes also called tongue-and-groove paneling. Made with narrow slats of wood, they are securely fitted together lengthwise. Used to form a strong and practical wall surface, this paneling was especially favored for utility areas, such as back porches or basement rooms, and was also commonly used as a ceiling surface for bungalow front porches.

85. Kitchen in Seattle, Washington. This kitchen is in a well-preserved 1914 bungalow built in the Mt. Baker neighborhood, an area which, like many other bungalow neighborhoods, developed after a streetcar line was extended to it from downtown. Designed by noted local architect Ellsworth Storey, it was featured in a 1916 issue of *Bungalow* magazine, which at that time was published in Seattle. Working closely with the well-researched ideas of the owners, it has been sensitively renovated to the design of local architect Joseph W. Greif, and it incorporates even more built-in conveniences than it had originally. Retaining the original kitchen's floorplan, the rather snug space of the breakfast nook is relieved by the ingenious built-in table, the top of which slides back for easier access to the benches. Once everyone is seated, the top is pulled out to its full length. To use the table as a worksurface between meals, the floor level of the nook was raised so that the tabletop would be level with the nearby countertops. What appear to be several built-in bins, an old standby in bungalow-kitchen cabinetry, are actually deep, pull-out drawers that are used for a surprising variety of functions. The drawer in the bench at the right slides out on heavy-duty tracks, and conveniently holds children's art supplies for use while meals are being prepared. The lid of the other bench lifts up for more storage. In the nook and above the sink the original windows were preserved, and their geometric divisions show an influence of the Prairie style. To match the rest of the cabinets, the dishwasher at the center has been disguised by a wood panel. Below the cooking space at left, the top handle controls a handy roll-out worksurface with legs, which measures 24" wide by 48" deep when fully extended. The other handle pulls out a pair of deep recycling containers, conveniently located near the back door that is just out of view to the left. (For other views of this house see figs. 86, 117.)

86. *(Opposite)* Another view of kitchen in Seattle, Washington. Awash in natural light from an added skylight, this view is taken from in front of the sink seen in figure 85. Because they had access to a copy of the 1916 *Bungalow* magazine in which the house appeared, the owners and their architect were able to study the original floorplan and several interior photographs, which strongly influenced the development of the current design, which gives open space a high priority. Adapted from an Arts and Crafts period design by architect Joseph W. Greif, the small drop-leaf table, usually folded down and placed at one side of the room, provides flexibility as an easily movable extra worksurface. The floors were resurfaced in oak, and the kitchen hardware, which are reproductions of period designs, were chemically refinished by the owners from polished brass to their present aged patina. So as to not appear as a black hole at night, the new skylight was fitted with indirect, low-voltage lights in its shaft, and it also provides for ventilation in hot weather. The stylish doors on the china cabinet were inspired by the home's geometric window designs. The wall at the left includes a built-in oven at center, a small-appliance "garage" with a lift-up door at the left, a microwave hidden behind doors above the oven, and the refrigerator at far left.

87. Kitchen area in Spokane, Washington. Some bungalow owners may dream of a spacious, light-filled kitchen space like this, but few could create it out of the modest space they have to work with. Charmed by the Craftsman style and many features of bungalows, the owners decided that instead of trying to find all of their requirements in an existing house, they would build their own. With space and light both top priorities, they entrusted their project to Pasadena architect Doug Ewing, whose design represents a decidedly contemporary interpretation of the Craftsman style, with some references to the work of Greene and Greene (fig. 21). Viewed from a large open dining area, the kitchen area is awash in afternoon light, which streams across the hardwood floors through a study doorway to the right. Although the kitchen space is generous, it is well utilized by a functional layout and carefully planned built-ins. The stove, located in a commodious island, is screened from this view by a higher partition, which also supports a granite countertop, lined with four tall stools. Serving as the family's informal dining area, its central location saves many steps. The stools face a partly visible band of casement windows that are located above the sink wall. The large refrigerator at the right has been integrated into the rest of the cabinetry by its matching wood-panel facing. Facing the open dining area, a towering built-in sideboard, which matches the kitchen cabinets, is also fitted with a granite countertop. This narrow sideboard forms the end of a massive but open architectural division between the kitchen and the high-ceilinged living room to the left. Built into this division is a large cabinet, which stretches across the entire width of the opening. Its distinctive step-topped form was adapted from the built-in sideboard of the dining room in Pasadena's famous Gamble house, which was built in 1908 and designed by Greene and Greene. The cabinet, which is open to both sides of the division, incorporates back-to-back cupboard and drawer storage beneath the extra depth of its granite top. The broad opening above allows views from the kitchen to a huge, almost free-standing river-rock fireplace (fig. 37). Placed on either side of the opening, which is cased like a doorway, are a pair of Craftsman-style wall lights.

88. Kitchen in C. Hart Merriam house, Marin County, California. With walls and ceiling sheathed in their original native redwood, this kitchen exudes a warm and woodsy feeling appropriate to its rustic setting. Because the house is built on a hillside, the casement windows above the sink at right look outside to a deck area. Ringed by built-in benches, the deck serves as a spacious outdoor living area, and is part of the original design of the house, which was built in 1904 by a renowned naturalist and anthropologist. Access to the outside is through French doors in an angled bay-window-shape passageway that connects the kitchen to a large open living room and its soaring fireplace (fig. 29). The custom-made kitchen cabinets were detailed to harmonize with the simple board-and-batten style of the surrounding wood-work. Blending in well is the unusual hood over the stove, which has been clad in matching wood. Most of the upper cabinets are glass-fronted, and below each is an open shelf to accommodate the most frequently used items. For ease of maintenance, the countertops and backsplash have been surfaced with a handmade glazed tile, which forms an orderly grid pattern that defines the work areas. Providing a rather luxurious accent, as well as softness underfoot, a handsome Oriental carpet runner parallels the far wall. (For other views of this house see figs. 29, 75, 104, 105, 114.)

(Overleaf) 89. Kitchen area in Marin County, California. The meticulous design approach apparent in the remodeling of this bungalow's kitchen was clearly not driven by a goal to recreate what had once existed. Instead, now elegantly garbed in Arts and Crafts-style clothing, the kitchen exudes the owner's love and enthusiasm for designs of the period. Hanging over a Gustav Stickley library table, now used in the breakfast area, is one of the owner's unusual period lighting fixtures. Featuring sinuous metalwork overlays in a stylized dogwood pattern, it is a large, octagonal art-glass bowl from which hang four single lights. Adapted from a period design, the hand-crafted copper hood above the stove was commissioned for this room. Used as accents in the tile backsplash below it, a collection of period wall tiles made by California Art Tile of Richmond, California, depict scenes of that state's early missions. Quarter-sawn oak was used for all of the room's woodwork and cabinets. With a lighter stain, the same material was used for the flooring, which is inset with contrasting walnut accent strips. Attached to the ceiling by wood elements that recall Prairie style forms, the hanging cabinet has glass doors on either side to allow light to pass through, and for easier access. All the glass used in the upper cabinet doors is of the "wobble" variety, retrieved from an archi-tectural salvage business. A surprising touch of color is added by the tiny squares in each of its pierced backplates of the copper hardware, which have insets of green glass recessed behind them. On the countertop at center is a china coffee service in a reissued Roycroft pattern. Textiles recreated to match Arts and Crafts designs are used on the table under a Rookwood vase, disregard ink mark here and on the Roman shades of the French doors at left, which open to a small deck.

90. Kitchen in Oakland, California. Added to the rear of a 1910 house, this completely new kitchen was built to the design of Glen Jarvis of Jarvis Architects. At once sleekly contemporary and with Arts and Crafts styling, most of its design inspiration was taken from the adjoining original dining room, from which this view was taken (fig. 88). These two rooms are connected by a wide pocket door that duplicates an original door that connects the dining and living rooms. The kitchen's quarter-sawn white oak flooring and its Douglas fir woodwork and cabinets replicate the originals in the adjacent rooms. A contemporary note is the extensive use of granite countertops. A playful touch is seen at the left in the jagged outline of the backsplash, which was intended to simulate in miniature the skyline of a mountain range. Although it is a built-in element, the granite-topped island at the center was purposely made to resemble a piece of freestanding furniture. At the right the informal dining area is in an open alcove. The French doors at right lead to a deck with built-in seating, which may also be reached from the dining room. Arranged to form a broad, angled bay window above the sink, the band of new casement windows on the far wall offer a pleasant view of the rear garden. Showing how they are in perfect harmony with the Arts and Crafts style, a small group of Japanese objects are displayed in the foreground. Resting on a low tansu chest is a handsome red-orange lacquer box, and a cast-iron teapot sits on a small chest of drawers. (For other views of this house see figs. 23, 28, 75.)

The Bedroom
PRIVATE RETREAT

In a house as small as most bungalows, personal privacy was a precious commodity. Despite their frequent use of shared, multipurpose spaces and open vistas between primary rooms, most bungalow floor plans included separate bedrooms. Yet it was an expression of their practical planning that space was allotted where it would do the most good; the bungalow designer's rule of thumb was that most of the available space had to go to the living and dining rooms. This economical formula worked, and was an integral part of the bungalow's success story.

More so than in most other houses, bungalow bedrooms were coveted as a place of escape from the rest of the household. Space permitting, an ideal floor plan would include a short hallway, leading to the bedrooms and bath, and forming a buffer from the main living spaces (figs. 6, 11). Sometimes a bedroom was designed with access from two different directions, thus allowing its use to vary (fig. 11). As befitting a house with a reputation for convenience, bungalow bedrooms were always placed close to the bathroom (figs. 5, 6, 7, 8, 9, 10, 11), and sometimes one or more also adjoined it directly (fig. 9). Bedrooms were placed on a corner of the house whenever possible to allow for the greatest amount of light and good ventilation (figs. 6, 9, 10, 11). If enough corners weren't available, a double or triple window would be used (fig. 11). Bay windows, which usually accommodated at least three separate window openings, were also found in some bedrooms (fig. 9). These were sometimes fitted with built-in windowseats that lifted up for additional storage (figs. 100, 103, 104). Bedrooms were also expected to have closets, which could range from the bare minimum to a walk-in size, with its own window to keep clothing aired (fig. 11). Some closets had built-in shelves or drawer units to relieve the need for a bureau (figs. 8, 10, 11). While not typical, some bedrooms were built with direct access to the outside, and

some have been remodeled to provide it (fig. 110). Sometimes second-floor bedrooms opened onto a balcony, perhaps notched into the bungalow's roofline (fig. 99), across a gable front (fig. 103), or as an extension of a dormer.

Most bungalows housed families with children, and it was sometimes a challenge to accommodate them. Some secondary rooms, perhaps originally designated as a den or breakfast room, were sometimes turned into nurseries, bedrooms, or even playrooms. It was very much in fashion to give attention to creating appropriate children's environments that would foster creative play and learning skills (figs. 107, 108, 109). Always eager to point out and promote family-enhancing activities, *The Craftsman* magazine published ideas and drawings that dealt specifically with this subject. With a nursery design scheme published in August 1905, it suggested that a blackboard could be built between some of the vertical battens in a nursery's wainscot "within the reach of the little ones," an idea that still sounds good. Other popular design-advice books and magazines, many of which were aimed at a higher-end market than that of the average bungalow owner, still had a significant effect on determining ordinary middle-class taste. Manufacturers of home furnishings, especially furniture and wallcoverings, were quick to answer the need, and targeted a host of appealing products for the nursery and children's room (fig. 109). Their quality and inventiveness bear close scrutiny for contemporary applications (figs. 107, 108, 109).

With more than one child in the house and only two bedrooms in the typical bungalow plan, it was likely that bedroom space would have to be shared by siblings. If the home's roofline and the family budget permitted, many a child's only hope of a separate bedroom hinged on the availability of an expandable attic. If not built into a fin-

91. Scheme for a bedroom. This illustration appeared in a book called *Your Home and Its Decoration*, which was published in 1910 by the Sherwin-Williams Paint Company. A self-proclaimed "series of practical suggestions for the painting, decorating and furnishing of the house," it was compiled by the firm's Decorative Department. The omission of wallpaper from the book reflects the keen competition between paint and wallpaper manufacturers. The fashion for white-painted woodwork in bedrooms extends to the furniture, which has simple lines but is more influenced by the Colonial Revival style than by Craftsman. Between the crown and picture moldings, a stenciled design of stylized leaves and flowers forms an effective frieze. The central floral element is quite similar to the Glasgow rose, a design motif associated with the famous Scottish architect/artist Charles Rennie Mackintosh. The subtly mottled walls of this room in soft yellow-green are intended to represent a special hand-painted finish of multiple blended colors that is sometimes referred to as a "Tiffany finish." Both the bed linens and the wide border of the area rug repeat the colors of the frieze, and the rug's solid field ties in with the color of the walls.

92. Scheme for a bedroom. This 1910 bedroom was probably designed by the same person who was responsible for the room depicted in figure 78, for it appeared in the same book, *Your Home and Its Decoration*. A scheme of pale orange-yellow walls below a cream-color ceiling and frieze makes a pleasing and restful combination with the white woodwork. Instead of a wide frieze design, there is a narrow stenciled border, placed just above the picture molding. While all the pieces have rather simple lines, only the forms of the bed and dresser specifically suggest the Craftsman style. Consistent with Arts and Crafts taste, hand-decorated textiles that coordinate with the room's scheme are seen on the small table at left and on the bureau. Surrounding the pale green field of the rug, the deeper greens and orange-yellows of its border suggest a stylized landscape design similar to those that were used for friezes in Craftsman-style homes.

ished space from the start, bungalow attic spaces were often designed with the option of some future development. This was often a strong selling point. There was logical appeal in paying for only as much house as one's initial needs dictated. Yet, having built-in expansion space waiting upstairs as the family grew or grew up reduced the likelihood of having to relocate to larger, and more costly, quarters. If the house was planned for attic expansion, there was usually a staircase built into it from the start. If not, the most thoughtful bungalow plans anticipated this

need by providing a logical space for one to be installed later. During bad weather, many accessible but unfinished attic spaces formed spacious children's playrooms.

Rather than the visible stairway of the typical two-story house, most bungalows, although variations existed, tended to have staircases that were built between two walls and closed off by a door. Because of space restrictions, it was also common to find unusually steep staircases. Some houses reached their attics by employing the space-saving, pull-down stair-ladder installed in a hallway ceiling.

93. Built-in bench, concealing a disappearing "fresh-air" bed (shown closed). This appears to be a high-backed Craftsman-style built-in bench below three small windows. Installed in an outside wall of a Craftsman home in the West Adams district of Los Angeles, this is a rare and highly specialized example of a "patent-furniture" design that cleverly incorporates a double bed. A popular category of Victorian invention was that of folding or so-called disappearing furniture geared to solve domestic-space problems, which inevitably included the concealment of beds. Typical of these solutions was the wardrobe or armoire where the door opened to reveal a drop-down bed. This example hides a bed that is set into its own screened chamber, which, with a simple sliding mechanism resembling that of a bread-box lid, opens to the outside air. Probably dating from the Teens, the scarcity of this curiously designed bed suggests it was not a popular solution to the problem of space saving.

94. Built-in bench, concealing a disappearing "fresh air" bed (shown open). The mechanism that conceals the stationary bed is a fairly simple system of sequentially sliding and hinged wood panels. Fitted within a framed opening, this entire bed assembly was intended to be installed in any outside wall of the house. This particular example is located on the second floor, with adequate privacy lent by surrounding trees. This bed's appeal was marketed as a convenient way to realize the beneficial effects of a sleeping porch in areas which otherwise couldn't accommodate them. It represents the apogee of the space-saving obsession that is associated with bungalows.

Obviously not intended for daily use, these were most often found in houses whose attics would only be used for storage.

As an essential component of the finished outside appearance of numerous house designs, attic dormer or gable-end windows would generally be built in place. Whether or not their windows opened to finished rooms, they at least allowed some light and good air circulation for storage areas.

Second-floor attic spaces were not used just for bedrooms, playrooms, or storage areas. One of their most popular uses was as a sleeping porch, which sometimes adjoined an upstairs bedroom (fig. 11). These were spaces used for open-air sleeping, popularized by the belief that fresh air was a key to good health, and could even help cure certain respiratory ailments. In attics, they were often fitted into the open end of a gable peak (fig. 105). Because of their indoor-outdoor character and exposure to moisture in the air, their walls and ceilings were frequently covered, in lieu of plaster, with bead-board (sometimes called tongue-and-groove paneling), a durable surface of narrow, tightly fitted slats of wood, which was usually either varnished or painted. Floors were plain painted or stained fir planks, sometimes covered with grass matting, oilcloth, or perhaps linoleum for a bit of style and color. Furnishings were spartan by necessity, as most sleeping porches were rather compact and generally were intended to accommodate at least two beds. Under these circumstances, simple metal-framed cots were about all that would fit. While more commonly found in attics, because there was usually more space there, sleeping porches were also incorporated into first-floor areas. There they usually adjoined one or more bedrooms. If there was no other spot for one, using a screened-in front porch was the only option for some households. As their popularity waned, many sleeping porches were eventually converted to heated interior rooms, and new uses were never difficult to determine for them.

Bungalows became known for their use of innovative built-in furniture to save space, and the most celebrated examples have been the various forms of the disappearing bed (figs. 93, 94, 95, 96, 97). As a newly perfected and modern convenience of many bungalow floor plans, disappearing beds were most popular for occasional rather than daily use. They were ideal for rooms that might have dual uses, thus making conversion to a guest room almost instantaneous. Such beds were also marketed for the single-room units of many residential hotels and apartments, which, concurrent with the rise of the bungalow, were proliferating in most American cities.

For those who have been accustomed to the extra size or amenities of master bedrooms, that is the area of the bungalow most prone to the remodeling temptation. Some have combined two smaller bedrooms, or at least borrowed space from another, to provide larger owner's quarters (figs. 101, 110). Sometimes an additional bathroom has been added (figs. 102, 103). Others have taken over the entire attic as a master bedroom suite, adding a bathroom there and creating generous closet spaces.

The subject of bedroom decoration, as it was originally conceived, was in great contrast to the more robust color and texture recommended for the main living spaces. Design-advice sources of the day suggested that as restful retreats bedrooms should be bright and cheerful spaces, with a simpler quality than the main living spaces (figs. 91, 92). The decidedly feminine quality of the softer, lighter color palette deemed appropriate for the bedroom was thought to present a pleasing contrast to the more masculine character of the darkly stained woodwork and deeper colors of most bungalow living and dining rooms. This shift to a paler color scheme might also be extended into the hallway leading to the bedrooms, as it usually had no source of natural light except that which came through the various doorways.

It was generally recommended that the woodwork of the bedroom should be painted white or some pale color. The walls, if painted, were likely to be a soft shade such as golden yellow, pale green, soft blue, rose, or lavender-gray, sometimes called French gray. Some people still preferred to have in the bedroom the darkly stained woodwork of their living and dining rooms (fig. 99). Indeed, some early bungalows were built with all-wood interiors including the bedrooms (figs. 100, 103, 104). However, in the majority of bungalow bedrooms, a paler palette seemed to be preferred. This effect was also achieved by using lightly scaled furniture and accessories, and sometimes included simple inexpensive pieces entirely painted in white to match the woodwork (figs. 91, 92). By the Twenties, according to the popular home magazines, it was increasingly fashionable for middle-class bedrooms, including those in bungalows, to be furnished with matching suites of department-store Colonial Revival-style furniture.

Regardless of its furnishings, and because it was less likely to have the interesting woodwork seen in the main living spaces, the bungalow bedroom was always a prime candidate for using wallpaper. For wallpaper patterns in bedrooms, the most perennially popular motifs were tapestry-types or rather large-scale florals. These were often combined with matching friezes or smaller borders, sometimes with a simple overall ceiling paper. Many of the designs were loosely adapted from eighteenth-century patterns favored by the Colonial Revival style. Simple and stylishly tailored striped papers, sometimes printed to look like satin, appealed to those who wished to avoid floral complexity. However, such a plain pattern might be enlivened by a beribboned and flowery frieze. Many such

95. Built-in disappearing "Murphy bed." Of all the disappearing built-in beds, variations on this type have been the most popular. Originally named for its manufacturer, the name Murphy has subsequently been used to describe similar beds made by others. Much of its appeal was in its mechanical simplicity, which consisted of a sturdy hinge arrangement at one end of the bed, with which it could pivot from the stored vertical position. This particular example is in Seattle's Mt. Baker neighborhood in a 1911 house, where the bed unit is incorporated into a commodious room-wide wall of built-in storage cupboards and drawers. When closed, the bed is disguised behind a large, full-height dressing mirror framed by wood moldings. Only the pair of metal legs, which lie flush with the surface when it is vertical, betray its true function. These legs also function as handles to help disengage the unit from its wall pocket and lower it. There were many variations on this drop-down bed concept. A particularly common model was bolted to the back of a wide closet door, which was swung open before the bed could be lowered.

96, 97. Built-in disappearing "pull-out" bed (closed and open). Enclosed behind a wood facing that was intended to look like built-in drawers and a cupboard, this bed unit is set into the wall. An original feature of the 1908 Charles Warren Brown house in Santa Monica, California, its mechanics are quite simple. Attached to the wood panel, a heavy metal frame supports springs, mattress, and bedding but it rests on heavy-duty rollers. This type of disappearing bed relies on there being sufficient space behind the wall to accommodate it. It was usually designed to slide beneath other built-ins in adjacent rooms. In this example, the bed slides beneath a stairway and landing to the second floor. The concealing end panel could be readily designed to blend in with many types of built-in cabinetry. Allowing immediate conversion to a guest room when needed, this particular bed was used in a den, where it may have also been hidden beneath a built-in desk. (For other views of this house see figs. 47, 99.)

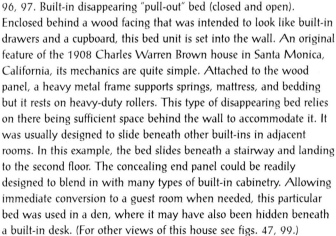

95

98. Bedroom in Mariposa (formerly the Frost-Tufts house), Hollywood, California. The shallow pitch of a gable's roof gives this bedroom ceiling its form. The room's windows are fitted with casement-type screens, hinged to swing into the room, and a natural linen Roman shade is attached to each. The room, furnished with dark-stained oak Roycroft furniture of the period, includes the "Marshall Wilder" chair and table, a pair of slatted single beds, and two matching bureaus with mirrors. On the bedside table is a small copper Roycroft lamp and a Roycroft American Beauty copper vase is on the bureau at left. A vintage clip-on reading light is attached to the bed. The simple white glass ceiling fixture is original to the house. Also of the period is the oak and leather Morris chair manufactured by the J.M. Young Company, one of Stickley's many competitors. A Navajo rug and colorful vintage blankets lend warmth to the room. In the event of a warm and still night a reproduction of a period electric fan stands on the bureau and is ready to keep the air moving. The plaster of the walls and ceiling was given a "sand-finish" treatment that was popular in the period. (For other views of this house see fig. 61 and figs. 84–91 in *The Bungalow*.)

friezes were specially die-cut to be découpaged over the wallpaper pattern, and some were also deeply embossed. Sometimes the low relief of embossed papers was given a striking dimensional quality with subtly shaded color.

The bungalow bedroom allowed the widest variety of furnishings and decorative treatments in the house. It could range from a random assemblage of functional cast-offs to a stylish and fashionable design statement. This flexibility of choice remains with us, and the bedroom is one of the last frontiers for experimenting with new design ideas in a self-contained and private space.

99. Bedroom in the Charles Warren Brown house, Santa Monica, California. A pair of French doors at the far end of a large second-floor bedroom in this 1908 house opens onto a small balcony, which is notched into the forward slope of a sweeping roof. Made of a blend of natural flax and linen, the curtains throughout the room are hand-embroidered and appliquéd with a ginkgo design adapted from one by Gustav Stickley. A door to a large closet is at the left of the French doors, and a matching closet at the right creates a recessed dressing alcove. A Limbert hall chair with striking tapered lines and pierced back and legs sits immediately to the left of the French doors. Enhancing the color of the stained fir woodwork, rosy-mauve painted walls make a simple but warm background. Against the side of the closet is an early Gustav Stickley bureau with a pivoting mirror. The substantial quarter-sawn oak bed was custom-made to a design by the current owner, who was inspired by Stickley. The small chest of drawers used as a nightstand is a reissued Stickley design. The period bedside lamp was made by Benedict Studios, who were also responsible for the manufacture of hardware used by Gustav Stickley in his furniture production. (For other views of this house see figs. 47, 96, 97.)

100. Bedroom in the Lillian Bridgman house, Berkeley, California. An early and rustic expression of the Craftsman taste, this 1899 house is named for its original owner-designer. The renowned Bay Area architect, Bernard Maybeck (1862–1957), urged Bridgman to design her own home, and is known to have given her some guidance. She also designed a studio at the rear of the property in 1908, which became her architectural office. Prior to that, she was a nationally published poet and writer of short stories, as well as a physics and chemistry teacher. Because the interior of this house was almost entirely finished in natural redwood, which provided glowing color and texture, there was little need to consider other finishes. This bedroom is located on the second floor, and its ingenious built-ins help to offset its small size. Under a pair of casement windows at left there is a windowseat with lift-up access to storage, and there is a built-in bureau cupboard tucked beneath the diminutive open staircase, which leads to an attic storage loft. A lift-up hatch, with a flush-mounted pull, provides more storage in the floor of the staircase landing. A small clinker-brick fireplace is angled across a corner at the right and above its shallow mantel a stepped pyramid of bricks forms an unusual juxtaposition with the exposed chimney, which is turned square with the room. The simple board-and-batten walls and the exposed framing joists and floorboards of the attic level above contribute to the rustic feeling of the room. Exemplifying its ideals, the Bridgman house was the type promoted by Berkeley's influential Hillside Club, which was formed to promote the construction of homes that would blend in with the area's natural landscape. It is located in a neighborhood that was first developed as the Scenic Park Tract of the lower Berkeley hills.

101. Bedroom with sitting area in Berkeley, California. Made possible by combining two smaller rooms, an adjoining sitting area creates a luxurious master bedroom not at all typical of bungalow planning. Originally built in 1907–1908, the room was remodeled to suit the needs of the current owners. The furnishings are a creative blend of past and present. The pale color scheme of creamy white walls and woodwork is in accordance with what was considered appropriate for bedrooms of the period. Distinguishing the walls of the sitting area is an original high wainscot, above which has been placed a recent wallpaper adaptation of a William Morris pattern of stylized willow branches. Its soft, rosy colors are enlivened by a reflective background flecked with metallic gold. The plate rail of the wainscot allows for changeable displays of artwork. A vibrantly colored Persian runner hangs horizontally above the bed, and a small pillow on the bed reproduces a William Morris design. The wide cased opening connecting the two spaces is mounted with a new pair of wood and glass Craftsman-style wall lights. The copper-and-mica lamp on the right bedtable and the shade for the old copper lamp base on the left table were also recently hand-crafted. In the sitting area, at left, the handmade oak and copper floor lamp was commissioned by the owners. The handsome bed, custom designed and hand-crafted for this space, was created with specific input by the owners, who wished it to evoke a feeling of the English Arts and Crafts Movement. Its design was inspired by the work of Ernest Gimson and of Sidney and Ernest Barnsley, three English architects who had fallen under the spell of the Movement during its early development. Other Arts and Crafts-style pieces of the period include a Morris chair by L. & J.G. Stickley, which is upholstered in a reproduction William Morris fabric design and the substantial oak chest of drawers to the left of the bed. An English silver-and-enamel box by the important Liberty metal-and-jewelry designer Archibald Knox sits on a Stickley Brothers tabouret next to it.

102. Bedroom in Marin County, California. First built in 1905 as a summer house, the original plans indicated that this was the master bedroom. The spacious house was built for the owner of a large dairy ranch, who could afford more than the typical Craftsman-style bungalow. Most of its main living spaces are natural wood, but as was the fashion in many Craftsman homes, this bedroom has light-painted woodwork and simple detailing. The room incorporates the owner's favorite colors that make up a striking interpretation of the Arts and Crafts style. The cream-colored woodwork sets off painted walls of a soft purple, which is repeated in the bedcover. Linked directly with the woodwork color, the softly mottled background of the friezes helps to highlight the repeated hand-painted designs. Adapted from a motif published in *The Craftsman* magazine in 1905 that is attributed to Harvey Ellis, it shows an influence of English Arts and Crafts work. The room is dominated by an imposing English oak wardrobe that is fitted with splendid hand-wrought copper hardware and a full-height beveled mirror. Its flat-capped crown and hardware and flaring supports under each front corner of the crown and hardware suggest the influence of English Arts and Crafts architect and designer C.F.A. Voysey (1857–1941). The recently woven rug in the foreground, with its boldly stylized floral motifs and vibrant coloring, is also similar to some of Voysey's designs. It was adapted from a carpet attributed to The Silver Studio that was woven for Liberty in 1903. The studio's owner, Arthur Silver, was an important English designer of the late nineteenth and early twentieth century, who did many textile and wallpaper designs that were marketed through Liberty's famous London store. Other Arts and Crafts furnishings include a pair of oak side chairs with caned seats and a hexagonal tabouret with pierced legs. The brass ceiling fixture and wall sconces are of the period. Simple Roman shades, made of a striped tone-on-tone fabric, are used on the multipaned casement windows and the French door in the center, which leads to a walk-in closet.

103. Bedroom in Berkeley, California. This attic room was original to this 1905 owner-designed house, and its amenities suggest that it was intended as the master bedroom. A small painted brick fireplace abuts the front wall of the building. Across an Oriental carpet, the afternoon sun streams through a French door, which leads to a small outside balcony. Sheltered by the deep eaves of the front-facing gable of the house, the balcony is entwined by an old wisteria, which has been trained up the façade. Wisteria was a favorite vine of the period; its fast growing suited the line-softening needs of Craftsman-style pergolas and porches. Its dangling clusters of fragrant blooms inspired many period textile, stencil, and wallpaper motifs. At the left, visible across the bed, an original built-in windowseat is set in a wide dormer beneath a double casement window. To provide more light and ventilation the large recently installed skylight fits between the original roof joists. Except for the hardwood floor, the room is entirely finished in natural redwood, and the walls feature board-and-batten paneling. Chosen for both the interior and some exterior surfaces of this house, redwood was favored locally for its durability and pest resistance, and is typical of other early examples of Craftsman-influenced Bay Area houses. (For another view of this house see figure 30.)

(Overleaf) 104. Guesthouse of the C. Hart Merriam house, San Francisco Bay Area, California. Evoking the image of a summer-camp cabin set in the woods, this all-redwood structure was designed by the current owner, and it replaces one that had been completely destroyed by a fire. Every board and beam that was used in this building was hand-selected by the owner, who personally supervised every phase of the project and worked closely with only two highly skilled craftspeople over a nine-month period. The opportunity for new construction allowed the inclusion of features that greatly enhance the building's use. The windows open onto a small covered porch, the flooring of which conceals a heated spa, which is easily entered through a hinged, lift-up section of the decking that folds out of the way to one side. Entry is through a Dutch door, visible in its half-open position at left. Next to it, vertical open shelving holds towels and robes for guests within handy reach of either the spa or the bathroom. The ladder leads to a small loft that is very popular with children. A pair of dark-stained Craftsman-style beds are enlivened by the bright red and black Hudson's Bay blankets. At the foot of each bed, a large blanket chest in a distressed green painted finish provides a lively color accent. This photograph was taken from a corner sitting area, where two sofa beds provide additional sleeping space. (For other views of this house see figs. 29, 75, 89, 105, 114.)

106. Sleeping porch in Los Angeles, California. A rare and untouched survivor dating from 1906, this sleeping porch remains fully open to the world outside. Because of insects, it was usual for such spaces to have been fitted with screens, but there is no evidence that any were ever installed here. Such amenities as a relative lack of insects, low cost of living, and mild climate helped establish Southern California as the bungalow mecca of America. This space probably survived because the roof overhangs help keep the elements at bay. Its wall and ceiling areas are durably surfaced in painted bead-board, also called tongue-and-groove paneling. Appropriate for its casual use, and consistent with period recommendations, the wooden floor is painted and covered by a simple sisal mat. Instead of the cots that might have originally furnished the space, a woven rope hammock is now suspended across one side. Pillows and blankets enhance the hammock's comfort and also that of the caned teak armchair, which was recreated from a nineteenth-century model. It is of a type originally found on shady verandas in the tropical reaches of the British Empire.

105. (Opposite) Sleeping porch in the C. Hart Merriam house, San Francisco Bay Area, California. Originally enclosed only by screens when the house was first built in 1904, this sleeping porch spans part of the roof's prominent side-facing gable. Unpainted natural redwood was used for the room's board-and-batten walls and peaked ceiling. The band of casement windows extends the length of the room, bringing in ample light, air, and views of the hillside property. The whimsical and highly personal design of the bed was created by the current owner, who also handpainted it with scenes of nature. Each post supports a wooden bear, handcarved in Japan, and each is in a different posture. The owner is also a textile artist who designed and made the bright quilt. A compact space, the sleeping porch has only room at this end for the bed, and a work area to accommodate the owner's drawing and painting activities is at the other. (For other views of this house see figures 29, 75, 89, 104, 114.)

107 *(Opposite)*, 108 *(Right)*. Children's playroom in Los Angeles, California. Remaining just as it was when first installed in the Twenties, the remarkably preserved state of this vintage wallpaper scheme for a children's playroom is exceedingly rare. While not original to the house, it is part of a surviving redecoration scheme that was undertaken in the Twenties. Located in Victoria Park, the house was built in 1911 and designed by the local architectural firm of Train and Williams. A rather narrow room, it is made to feel larger by its proximity to an outside deck, which is reached through French doors at the left. All of the wall, frieze, and ceiling areas were covered with a plain oatmeal paper, which provides a background of subtly mottled texture and a warm neutral color. Popular in the early twentieth century, oatmeal papers were often used alone as in the ceiling and walls of this room, or as the plain ground for patterns printed over them. Above the picture molding a series of printed wallpaper panels is placed at regular intervals. Each of these was découpaged on the background paper to form a frieze around the room, and the panels illustrate families visiting a zoo. In addition, a beautifully colorful wallpaper panel of delphinium (also called larkspur) has been set in the recessed panel of each door. The flower panels were printed on background paper matching the plain stock used elsewhere. The room displays a suitable collection of children's vintage toys and stuffed animals. The painted side chair, with its turned legs and decorated splat, is typical of so-called cottage furniture that was popular for kitchens and bedrooms in the Twenties. At right, what appears to be a large oak cabinet houses a variation of the "disappearing bed." A freestanding piece, rather than a built-in, this example is closer in design to eclectic styles of the Victorian era, whose influence on public taste lingered well into the early twentieth century.

109. Wallpaper designs for a nursery. The topic of children's rooms, of perennial concern for any family with youngsters, was a popular subject in design-advice books and periodicals of the early twentieth century. At the time, because of increased public awareness of various behavioral and educational issues related to child rearing, there was a growing middle-class concern for what made a suitable environment for children. Articles in home magazines discussed what was best for children, from decoration and furniture to toys and games. For many people, it became fashionable to be very conscious of how such things might affect a child's development and learning abilities. How this concern was expressed in the home became an opportunity to show one's social sophistication. As a result, children's rooms developed into a specialized market niche that manufacturers became quite adept at accommodating. This corner detail of a proposed wall treatment in a nursery features three wallpaper borders that were offered in the 1916–1917 catalog of James Davis Artistic Paperhangings of Chicago. While each border could be used independently of the others, the point of this illustration was to encourage using all three together for the best effect because "children like quantity." At the lower part of the wall, there is a plain background paper on which various colorful prints of animals, called "Animal Cutouts," have been separately découpaged. Unlike the cutout animals, the "Child World Frieze" above them was a printed scene of children in the country. Above them, the third border on the upper wall is also made with découpage. Cutout children's figures taken from the separately printed "Nursery Rhymes Frieze" are overlaid on a striped ground. Each panel is framed with twining ribbons and flower clusters.

110. Bedroom in Marin County, California. Sleek horizontal lines inspired by Prairie School architecture distinguish this spacious room, which the current owner enlarged to make a master bedroom, as part of an extensive renovation. Part of its space was taken from a smaller bedroom, and the remainder of that bedroom was turned into a large walk-in closet, out of view to the left. Through a doorway at the right is a separate dressing room, more closet space, and an additional new bathroom (fig. 121). At the end of the room a new pair of French doors provides access to a rear garden area. Period lighting collected by the owner is used throughout the house, and this room is lit by unusual examples. The square brass ceiling fixture, flush-mounted to the ceiling, has a leaded, Prairie-style geometric art-glass shade. The striking leaded art-glass wall sconces were made from a design by famed Chicago architect Louis Sullivan (1856–1924), whose early work in steel-frame high-rise construction earned him renown as the father of the modern American skyscraper. Sullivan is also celebrated for his genius in designing architectural ornament. Near the left corner is a Limbert "cut-out" rocker, and next to it the curving top of a Gustav Stickley scrap basket is visible. On the wall above is an early view of San Rafael by noted California painter William Keith, one of the most successful and admired Bay Area painters of the late nineteenth and early twentieth centuries. On the night stand at the left are a Heintz art-metal vase and a rare Heintz picture frame, both with silver overlay on bronze. King-size, the bed has a substantial architectural quality. Its densely slatted headboard and footboard, anchored by square capped newel-like posts, recall a Prairie-style stair railing. The delicately patterned geometric bedcover and its pillow shams were made in Austria. The fabric is a reissued period pattern of the Wiener Werkstätte, a Viennese firm (1903–1932) that was famous for its progressive decorative arts. (For other views of this house see illustration facing page 1 and figs. 69, 87, 120, 121.)

The Bathroom
CONVENIENCE ENSHRINED

The design of the American bathroom was largely determined by emerging advances in technology. Bungalows were veritable proving grounds for some of the more progressive bathroom concepts. During the last quarter of the nineteenth century, indoor plumbing had become commonplace in the majority of middle-class homes that were located in or near cities. But these Victorian conveniences were far from the gleaming, streamlined models they were destined to become in the twentieth century. Because industrial development near cities spawned many bungalow tracts, some of their first inhabitants were recent converts from an agricultural to an industrial-based livelihood. For some of these people a bungalow provided them with their first indoor bathroom. And so the legend of the bungalow as being the most modern house of its day continued to grow.

The utilitarian image of the middle-class bathroom was slow to change from the relative austerity that recalled its nineteenth-century origin. When entering a turn-of-the-century bathroom, what struck one first were the plumbing fixtures. Most of these were utilitarian, without much sense of style. However, innovations in fixture design that would make them more attractive as well as practical were already well underway. Even the finest bathrooms in the nation's wealthiest households were not that different in basic amenities from the middle-class bathroom, except perhaps in their size and finishes. Bathrooms looked remarkably the same for many years before and after the turn of the century (fig. 111). White porcelain-finished fixtures were standard until the Twenties, when they began to be used in combination with colored ceramic tiles (fig. 112). Soon, matching colored porcelain fixtures began to be marketed by manufacturers. For the average household, however, colorful bathrooms didn't become familiar until the Thirties (figs. 116, 117).

When the bungalow emerged, the classic footed, porcelain-enameled cast-iron tub was the most standard bathroom fixture across the country (figs. 114, 121). The most typical shape of its feet—a claw clutching a ball—was adapted from eighteenth-century English and American Colonial furniture in the Chippendale style.

Eventually eclipsing footed tubs entirely because of the difficulty in cleaning under and behind the tub, were models that were installed flush to the floor and against the wall. This form still persists today as the accepted modern standard for bathtubs (fig. 119). While the most up-to-date and affluent of early twentieth-century households could have obtained an early version of the enclosed tub before 1910, it did not reach the average household until much later. A step in the right direction was the pedestal tub, which was also of cast iron and freestanding from the wall, but gracefully enclosed at the bottom to form the solid base that inspired its name (figs. 111, 115). These often had plumbing attachments in the center of the long side. While an attractive alternative, pedestal tubs were enormously heavy and expensive. Also expensive and developed around the same time were cast-iron tubs shaped to abut the walls without a gap and sit flush to the floor. By the Twenties, a common stop-gap solution was to box in old footed tubs in an attempt to modernize them. This was done by enclosing them with wood panels on the outer sides, which were then frequently covered in ceramic tile, with the area around the top of the tub also patched in. This was seldom a long-term or aesthetically satisfying solution. Even before the arrival of colored bathroom fixtures, there were better and cheaper enclosed tubs on the market. These became the standard fare for new bathrooms and usually featured rounded lines. Showers were commonly built over them, with their plumbing now located inside the wall (fig. 112). Even from the early

111. Scheme for a bathroom. Appearing in a 1912 catalog published by the Eberson Paint Company, the purpose of this illustration was to show how the starkness of an all-white scheme of ceramic tile and plumbing fixtures could be relieved by using peach-color paint on the upper walls and ceiling. Also effective is the simple green and white stenciling just above the tile wainscot. Otherwise, this bathroom has the rather plain character usual to this period. The style of its fixtures suggests that the illustration was portraying an upscale bath rather than one that would fit a typical bungalow budget. For example, there is a pedestal tub instead of a footed tub, and the pedestal sink is shown with an elegant base in the form of a classical column. A pair of wall sconces, probably nickel-plated, light the mirror above the sink. The leaded-glass window above the tub in a popular period pattern was unusual for a bathroom. The small rug repeats the peach color of the walls and the green of the stenciling in its borders.

112. Scheme for a bathroom. By the late Twenties, color had finally become prominent in the American bathroom. This sun-splashed modern bathroom design was used in a 1927 magazine advertisement for a tile manufacturer. Although the sink and tub are still white, the room as a whole shows the importance of colored tile that covers the walls and encloses the tub. A line of narrow black tile underscores the lip of the tub and continues around the room. This accent is emphasized near the floor by a narrow strip of black and white tile that also continue around the walls. The built-in shower over the tub became the standard arrangement. The typical pedestal sink has a small shelf for toiletries mounted on the wall above it. The importance of color to the room scheme is emphasized by the pale rose of the walls and the deep plum of the rug borered in blue and white.

twentieth century, space permitting, more expensive bathrooms generally had a separate stall shower. The typical plumbing hardware for tubs hasn't changed greatly in the ensuing years. Then, as now, it allowed hot and cold water to be mixed together and attached showers were operated by simply pulling on a lever to divert the water flow upward.

Much early twentieth-century bathroom hardware was nickel-plated brass. Quite similar to a chrome finish, nickel plating has a silvery color, with a slightly warmer quality than that of chrome (figs. 114, 115). Chrome plating eventually surpassed nickel in popularity for its more modern look. While most bathroom fittings were made of brass and continue to be, it was more practical to plate them in a nickel or chrome finish, for either is much easier to clean and maintain. In remodelings, some prefer brass for purely aesthetic reasons (fig. 119), but the polished or sometimes brushed or satin finishes of chrome and nickel plating were most characteristic of the hardware in bungalow bathrooms.

Also made of cast iron in a glossy white porcelain finish, the bathroom sink was made in various forms and sizes. Freestanding pedestal sinks had been used since the late nineteenth century, and continued to be popular throughout the entire bungalow era. The bases of earlier models were sometimes made with vase-like shapes or the form of a classical column (figs. 111, 115). Most typical were sinks with smoothly rectangular forms and rounded edges (figs. 112, 114, 116, 117). Other types of the bathroom sink were all-porcelain models that were supported by front legs. Wall-mounted sinks were often used in bungalow bathrooms because they saved floor space, and were easier to clean under. Corner sinks were also popular, for even the most compact bathrooms could accommodate them. Hot and cold water faucets were often operated separately without blending their water together (fig. 115). By the Thirties, it became common for most households to have "mixer" fittings.

The wide range of toilets was partly a result of various patents for flushing mechanisms, which were held and produced by different manufacturers, for there was much competition in the plumbing-fixture business. Flushing-handle mechanisms ranged from push-down to pull-up levers. Some models even sported a "push-button" flushing action that was considered the height of modernity. Pull-chain toilets with tanks installed high on the wall for greater flushing power were Victorian holdovers that were still common and available in the early twentieth century. These were found in some of the earlier bungalows. There were plenty of more familiar toilet models available at the same time, which were considered more modern and attractive, as well as less noisy to flush and easier to clean. An unusual form was a toilet with a circular tank, nick-

named a "pillbox toilet." Varnished wooden seats were gradually replaced by ones manufactured with a lacquer-like enamel finish, which was considered more sanitary.

Once the issue of fixtures was resolved, the bathroom's floor and wall finishes were the next major consideration. Since most bungalows had only a single bath, it was essential that it be finished with very durable materials, which were easily maintained. A clean bathroom was a beautiful bathroom. The cheapest and most prevalent solution for the average bathroom was to coat it with a heavy-duty, white enamel paint. This made virtually every surface scrubbable. Such a simple treatment was also easy to freshen up with a new coat of paint when needed.

Many bungalow bathrooms had walls divided by a wooden chair-rail molding, which was usually placed about four to five feet up the wall (fig. 113). Subject to more abuse and moisture, and with a more frequent need to be cleaned, this lower wall area needed to be especially durable. Instead of there being only enameled plaster walls in this wainscot area, there was a common use of bead-board, also called tongue-and-groove paneling. It had been a popular and tough wall finish since the Victorian era, and continued to be an economical and serviceable solution in the bungalow bathroom. Another solution for the bath's lower walls was to cover them with sanitary wallpaper, which was expressly manufactured for such areas prone to dampness and frequent cleaning. So-called sanitaries were intended to be varnished after installation, in order to seal their surface for repeated washings. They were usually offered in tile-like patterns, and were an early vehicle for some color and pattern to appear in the bungalow bathroom. Changes in the manufacture and materials of modern wallcoverings have made them practical for remodeled baths (fig. 118).

Ceramic tile was the ideal choice for both floors and walls of bathrooms, not only in bungalows, but in virtually every other type of house. While, of course, more expensive than any of the other bathroom finishes discussed, it added to the value of the house because of its greater permanence (figs. 111, 112). Many vintage tiled bathrooms are as serviceable now as when they were installed, and still look just as good. The most-used flooring tile was of high-fired, unglazed porcelain, typically formed into tiny 1" x 1" hexagons. These interlocked into a tight-fitting, honeycomb-like pattern with extra-thin grout lines that were ground flush with the floor surface (figs. 114, 115). It makes a hard, non-skid surface, and when properly installed, is one of the most practical flooring solutions ever devised. It is all but indestructible, easily mopped or scrubbed, and blends with virtually any kind of decorative scheme. Typically all white, some floors were enlivened with one or more color accents, usually available in black, blue, green, ochre, or rose, which were placed to form

113. Built-in bathroom cabinet in Pasadena, California. Stretching from wall to wall, this built-in cabinet shows how much extra storage space a carefully planned bathroom could possess. An original feature of a 1911 bungalow, the cabinet includes ample cupboard space with shelves inside, especially handy for towel storage. Below each pair of small drawers, convenient for personal toiletries, are three additional wider drawers. At center, two deeper drawers form a useful built-in seat. In other arrangements, such a seat often lifted up to provide space for a laundry hamper. There are small casement windows at either side of the tall mirror. A pair of simple period wall lights is mounted on the window casings, and the mirror covers a door that encloses a generous medicine cabinet. Originally painted, the bathroom's woodwork was stripped and refinished, as part of a recent renovation by the current owners, and at the same time, unglazed terra-cotta pavers were installed on the floor. (For another view of this house see fig. 53.)

114. Bathroom in the C. Hart Merriam House, San Francisco Bay Area, California. In a white-on-white scheme that typifies the period, this bathroom has retained both its 1904 form and original claw-footed tub. Beneath their white enamel finish, the board-and-batten walls and the exposed ceiling structure are made of redwood. Located on the second floor, the placement of the two original casement windows reflects the sweeping line of a roof gable, which is indicated by the slope of the ceiling. This bathroom was subject to a recent renovation; the period-style toilet and pedestal sink are replacements, and all of the fixtures were fitted with new, appropriately styled nickel-plated hardware. The addition of a built-in linen storage compartment behind a drop-down door above the tub, now utilizes a previously walled-over space. The small hexagonal tiles recreate a typical bathroom floor of the period. The original owner and builder of this house carefully placed the tub to allow an uninterrupted view into the surrounding trees. (For other views of this house see figs. 29, 75, 89, 104, 105.)

115. (Opposite) Bathroom in the Henry Weaver house, Santa Monica, California. A testimonial to the enduring soundness of its original planning, this 1911 bungalow's bathroom has survived almost completely intact. Prominent among its features is the graceful pedestal tub. The original nickel-plated fittings at the center of one side characterize this particular type of fixture. The ample curves of the pedestal sink include a substantial, vase-shaped base, whose swelling form suggests an oversized baluster of a classical railing. Its nickel-plated hardware has the separate hot and cold faucets typical of the period. The toilet is located in the corner opposite the window, and a separate stall shower is in the corner to the left of the tub. The design of the original floor contains a combination of small hexagonal and square unglazed porcelain tiles enlivened by a Greek Key border. Extending about two-thirds of the way up the walls are the original 3" x 6" glazed tiles that are capped by a wood picture molding. A tall casement window is crowned by an unusual semicircular beveled-glass transom. Providing generous amounts of light and air, the window frames a splendid tangle of greenery. Made of dowel-shaped lengths of solid glass, the towel bars are elegant original touches. (For another view of this house see fig. 32.)

117. Bathroom in Seattle, Washington. This 1913 bungalow's spacious bathroom was first remodeled in the Thirties, and a recent remodeling retained the green plumbing fixtures. Even the sink's faucet handles are the same green. The linear divisions of the casement windows duplicate those of the originals; a distinctive design repeated elsewhere in the house. They were designed by Ellsworth Story, the noted local architect of the house, which was shown in Henry L. Wilson's *Bungalow Magazine* in 1916. The arch-top, built-in medicine cabinet survives from that time. The new ceramic tile is handmade and custom colored to harmonize with the vintage fixtures. In a stylized Art Deco floral pattern, a narrow low-relief border tops the tile wainscot. This particular shade of green, part of the Art Deco color palette, was popularized after the discovery of King Tutankhamen's tomb in 1922. It was sometimes even referred to as *Eau de Nil*, or "water of the Nile," and appeared in the enamel colors of kitchen appliances dating from the period. (For other views of this house see figs. 72, 73.)

116. *(Opposite)* Bathroom in Monrovia, California. Unchanged since it was added between a pair of attic-level bedrooms in the early Thirties, this fully tiled bathroom still packs a surprising wallop. It is a revealing example of the changing fashions in bathroom design that swept America in the later Twenties, and is striking testimony to the vogue for strongly colored bathroom tile and plumbing fixtures. This room's jazzy Art Deco style contrasts with the more conservative character of the rest of the house, which was built only about a decade earlier. Whoever was responsible for the design of this second bathroom chose to pursue the latest fashion. Because there are no windows, the use of black glazed tile is a surprising choice, and reeks more of glamour than practicality. The black tile does make an effective foil for the pale green of the pedestal sink, toilet, and tile accents, which are used to form a geometric border. Additional tile accents in a striking metallic gold glaze are used at the top of the walls. There is no bathtub, but instead a built-in stall shower is located at the right. Through the doorway and in front of the window is a rare Craftsman-style phonograph of the period.

widely spaced, repeating patterns. It was also popular, when affordable, to add decorative geometric borders created with small square tiles. One of the most popular borders was the Greek Key design (fig. 115). The wall surface most often accompanying this type of floor was made with 3" x 6" white glazed ceramic tiles. The height of this tiling was similar to the wainscot area mentioned earlier. Occasionally, some decorative tiles appeared as an accent or border trim, usually near the top of the wainscot area,

but sometimes elsewhere (figs. 112, 116, 117). A special ceramic trim piece with a profile like a wood molding was sometimes used to cap the top of the tile wainscot.

Many bungalow bathroom floors were simply finished in a softwood such as fir. Sometimes stained, such floors would generally be highly varnished for easier cleaning. If painted, it was recommended to use the kind of sturdy deck paint that might appear on the floor of utility areas, or perhaps even the front porch. These softwood floors

118. Bathroom in Portland, Oregon. This is one of two bathrooms that were recently remodeled in a bungalow located in the Laurelhurst Park neighborhood. This one on the first floor was designed to function as a guest bath. Working with Blackburn/Connolly Interiors its owners chose a design approach that was inspired by the period, but is in no sense a strict copy. Greenish-gray slate was chosen for the flooring and was also used to form a high baseboard. The diagonal placement of the slate squares helps to expand the feeling of space. A floral wallpaper, which would also be appropriate in a bedroom, extends from the top of the baseboard to a picture molding installed several inches below the ceiling. The pattern that transforms the space into a cheerful bower of honeysuckle is reproduced from one designed in 1883 by May Morris, the daughter of England's great William Morris. Its style is reminiscent of her father's famous wallpaper and textile patterns of the English Arts and Crafts period. Active in his firm, Morris & Company, May Morris was put in charge of its embroidery department in 1885, and she also designed some jewelry. Most of her design work was related to needlework rather than printed patterns such as wallpaper. The plumbing fixtures in this room were replaced during an earlier remodeling. Supported by a pair of chrome-plated legs, the sink and its hardware are rather modern in style, but are given a more vintage feeling by the addition of a ceramic-tile backsplash. A narrow panel of low-relief, gray-green tiles with a leaf design is framed with deep cream and they in turn are framed by white tiles. Out of view in the corner opposite the sink is a new shower that utilizes the same tile colors that appear in the sink's backsplash. A low wall, capped by a handy painted shelf, helps to screen the toilet, creating a separate compartment for it without blocking light. (For another view of this house see fig. 14.)

were often overlaid with linoleum. This enabled some pattern and additional color to be introduced, and patterns that imitated ceramic tile were most popular.

As elsewhere in bungalows, most bathrooms had some kind of built-in storage. The bare minimum, a medicine cabinet with a mirror, was usually placed above the sink (figs. 111, 112, 115, 117). The sink was often placed between two small windows that could be opened, which allowed even, natural light for the mirror (fig. 117). Natural light was usually supplemented by single wall-mounted fixtures (figs. 111, 115, 116, 117). If the bath-

room was large enough to require it, a ceiling fixture, such as a simple milk-glass shade suspended from a single chain, might be provided as a companion light. Besides cupboards for towels and drawers for toiletries, built-in storage might include a tall mirror and incorporate a seat, which often lifted up for laundry storage. To take up the least amount of space, the toilet was generally located in the same room as the sink and tub. However, some house plans featured a "split bath," which placed the toilet in its own separate space with a door and window.

119. Bathroom in the Oscar Maurer house, Berkeley, California. Although contained within a turn-of-the-century house, this compact bathroom is of entirely new construction, and was designed by John Zanakis/House of Orange. It shows a splendid inventive approach to creating a modern bathroom that is compatible with the period environment that exists just beyond its door. The design of the original board-and-batten wainscoting in the adjacent rooms was the inspiration for the unusual ceramic-tile wall treatment above the tub. The proportions of the woodwork wainscoting were precisely duplicated, using pieces of a dark brown matte-glazed tile. Narrow strips of tile, set to stand out from the larger background pieces, were cut to form the vertical "battens" and the horizontal top rail. Above the tile wainscot the walls are covered with large tiles in a mottled glaze. A short wall at right helps to separate the tub, and it is fitted with a period art-glass panel that includes a highly stylized California poppy. A similar panel, salvaged from the same house, was made into a casement window above the tub. Unplated period-style brass hardware, preferred here for its color harmony with the surrounding materials, is used throughout. The period rose-colored marble sink top was salvaged from another house, and set into a copper-lined surround and backsplash. At the right, hammered-copper period wall lights flank a framed mirror that conceals a built-in medicine cabinet. (For other views of this house see figs. 2, 26.)

120. Bathroom in Marin County, California. This bungalow's original bathroom has been elegantly refashioned by the owner's personal interpretation of the Arts and Crafts style. As with most houses of modest scale, available storage space was at a premium, so it was a priority to create as much of it as possible. Filling an entire wall, the extensive built-ins create a dramatic arch-top recess for the sink area. This bath can also function as a dressing room, for it incorporates roomy built-in bath, as well as linen storage. The hammered-copper hardware has a dark patina and was handmade from period designs. The recessed toespace helps make the cabinets appear less weighty and more furniture-like. Multiplied by the mirrored panel above the sink, a matching set of striking period light fixtures features geometric art-glass designs reflecting the Prairie style. Also glimpsed in the mirror, and suggesting a fanciful view through an open window, is a handpainted ceramic-tile mural of a Marin County landmark, Mt. Tamalpais. Only partially seen through its nickel-plated glass door, the mural covers the shower's entire back wall. (For other views of this house see the illustration facing page 1 and figs. 69, 74, 103, 121.)

121. (Opposite) Bathroom and dressing room in Marin County, California. Culminating in a luxuriously equipped master bathroom, seen through the second doorway, this sequence of spaces is entered directly from the master bedroom. Only a part of the extensive remodeling of a rather modest bungalow, this area was made possible by transforming existing space. The prevailing theme of the Arts and Crafts style was consistently emphasized by careful selections of finishes and woodwork detailing. Used in every room of the house, the owner's collection of fine period lighting gives each area another treasured focal point. The area of the master bedroom especially took its inspiration from elements of the Prairie style. In the left foreground, one of the master bedroom's rare art-glass wall lights, designed by famous Chicago architect Louis Sullivan, is visible. Below it, a striking period oak cabinet with slatted sides has an unusual inlaid panel of paired birds, executed in contrasting woods, on its cupboard door. On the shelf beneath it is a Tiffany "Pine Needle" inkwell of patinated copper. The other shelves hold a bronze Art Deco box and a tall Rookwood Pottery vase. Proceeding into the dressing room, one finds another pair of wall lights, matching those used in the bedroom, hanging at either side of the built-in dressing table, and above it is a four-light ceiling fixture with geometric art-glass shades in the Prairie style. Quarter-sawn oak was used for flooring, woodwork moldings, and built-in cabinetry. On the dressing room floor, corner inlay details executed in walnut strips form a geometric flourish that was popular in the early twentieth century. This particular design, used throughout this house, was adapted from floors in the owner's childhood family home, the architecture and features of which inspired a lifelong interest in the Arts and Crafts Movement. The chair, with the thin vertical slats of its back extending almost full height, was recently adapted from one by Frank Lloyd Wright. A prized Tiffany "ball" fixture illuminates the bathroom. In grand period style, a salvaged oversized tub has centrally mounted fittings in a nickel-plated finish, and its elaborate ball-and-claw feet were also plated. (For other views of this house see the illustration facing page 1 and figs. 69, 74, 103, 120.)

Before & After
ROOMS OF TRANSFORMATION

The following photographs are intended as inspirational testimonials. They may be considered as tools in the process of transforming a lackluster bungalow space into an inviting one. Although there is a calculated drama to their contrasts, these room makeovers didn't go as if by magic from A to Z. The photographs gloss over the inevitable and innumerable agonies and ecstasies. However, they do show that there is light at the end of the long restoration or remodeling tunnel. A two-way street, fixing up an old house can sometimes seem an endless, thankless task, but one of the best rewards is sharing a labor of love with others who truly understand and appreciate the effort. These rooms are not intended to fit every situation, but it helps to see what others have done. Perhaps they will inspire similar solutions, or trigger decisions to do things differently. At best, they might break up some log jams of indecision.

It is a daunting prospect to ponder the collective fate of the countless numbers of forlorn, neglected, abused, or simply dingy old bungalows, nationwide. Old houses that require attention, like people, are best considered on an individual basis. Every old house needs to find the right owner to love and care for it. Once so united, after the honeymoon is over, what to do next is a matter of prioritizing. At the top of most lists are the basic structural and building systems that affect soundness and safety. From the roof to the foundation, an old house, intricately interwoven with dubious electrical, heating, and plumbing systems, can present many problems. For those who accept the challenge, early discovery of this can be swift and merciless. Even a simple fix-up job can balloon into a nightmare, usually accompanied by much puzzling and indecision. Budget issues tend to be more clearcut: either it is affordable, or it will have to wait, or it can be done differently for less money. Although financial considerations can affect aesthetics, money doesn't necessarily solve everything. Making aesthetic decisions about one's home seems to present a universal, perennial dilemma.

A key to making sound decisions about revitalizing an old house is seeking good information. One of the best sources is to observe carefully and be alert for clues. Sometimes the problem has been solved long ago by someone else, and it just needs to be uncovered. House tours in revitalized old neighborhoods are popular sources for new approaches and ideas. Most old house interiors, including those of bungalows, are not in their original condition. In the rare instances when they are, they tell a revealing tale not only of period interior design, but about American life in the early twentieth century. Such nearly miraculous circumstances in a handful of treasured house museums are seen by relatively few people (figs. 81, 148, 149, 152–173). We are indeed fortunate that these remarkable time capsules are available for repeated public visits, study, and enjoyment. However, the elevated status of a protected historic landmark is shared by very few houses.

Even today, in an age when historic preservation is burgeoning, the fate of an old house is all too often in the hands of destiny. Even if found substantially intact, it is rarely possible or realistic to expect that every new owner will be obsessively strict about maintaining the original design scheme. There must be room for some concession to change, but change doesn't have to spell disaster. After all, the simple experience of living soon teaches us to accept change, welcome or not, as part of life. The same is true of old houses and original interiors. Armed with a realistic sense of expectation and inevitability, we can seek to learn as much as we possibly can about old houses before we change them. For many neglected houses, well-conceived changes can be their salvation, and increase their longevity.

Few old houses, especially after seven, eight, or more decades of service, have not been hit by the remodeling bug somewhere along the way. Because of the typical pattern of American urban development, most old houses have had multiple owners with widely varied personal and financial circumstances. Like those dating to the Victorian era, most bungalow neighborhoods have witnessed tremendous demographic changes since they were first developed. Many haven't been as well-loved and cared for since the days of their original proud occupants.

Fortunately, bungalows are part of the younger generation of old houses, which means that quite a few have slipped through remarkably unscathed. Although increasingly rare, some are still occupied by their original owners. Greater numbers of them have only changed hands once or twice. Such circumstances certainly raise the likelihood that fewer changes have taken place. This also suggests that the road to discovery about the history of the house could be a relatively short one.

Old house lovers are fascinated by who and what came

122. **Before:** Bungalow entry in San Jose, California. The dark stained and varnished fir woodwork of this 1908 house was well preserved, but its plaster walls had all been painted a harsh white. While less typical for a bungalow, the front door at right opens from the front porch into this small entry vestibule. The small window, which is on the side of the house and facing shrubbery, can open for ventilation. The built-in hall stand, complete with mirror, hooks, and space for umbrellas, is original, and obviates the need for any other furniture. At the left, a wide pocket door leads to the dining room. This house is in the Hanchett Park neighborhood, which was first developed in the early twentieth century, and is noted for its diverse collection of bungalow styles.

123. **After:** Bungalow entry in San Jose, California. The strong horizontal lines of the existing mahogany-stained woodwork are subdued and its color flattered by two period-style wallpapers. A landscape frieze was a popular way to introduce views of nature into the Arts and Crafts interior. In this example, a handsome pine tree, laden with metallic copper cones, repeats against an undulating background of water and mountains. Reproduced from a Jeffrey & Company pattern that was published in a 1911 English design periodical called *The Journal of Decorative Arts*, its rustic motif is at home in this American bungalow interior. Recreating a rich period effect, the ceiling glows with a metallic gold paper that has been overprinted with delicate intersecting lines to suggest the texture of burlap. Although such light-reflecting treatments sometimes employed real textiles with a gilded finish, the effects were more often achieved through the use of printed or embossed papers. Anchored by a substantial baseboard, the tailored stripes and subtle tone-on-tone wallpaper pattern in the natural colors of kraft paper suggest the effect of a high wainscot. Emphasized by the light, its wide vertical stripes are divided by delicately gilded chain-like lines.

before them. Beyond the mere novelty factor, such information can solve mysteries about changes, and perhaps illuminate the current owner's decision-making process. Occasionally, lucky new owners are able to obtain old photographs from former occupants. Besides allowing glimpses of the people who lived there, sometimes, in the background, eye-opening details, such as how they used the rooms, or arranged the furniture, are revealed. One of the circumstances most charged with the reality of the past

is to be able to talk to someone who lived there before. More often than might be expected, out of sheer sentimental attachment, former owners or occupants will ring the bell. They are also more likely to do so if the house is in a good state of repair. While subject to the whims of memory, even if isn't about how the house was decorated, something of interest will be gleaned from the exchange. Invariably, between bungalow lovers there is plenty of common ground.

124. **Before:** Details of the living room, and of the adjacent entry and dining room, San Jose, California. Inside the same house seen in figures 122 and 123, the stark contrast of white walls and dark stained woodwork extended into the living room in the foreground, and into the dining room, through the doorways at the left. The beveled mirror and form of the built-in hall stand are more visible in this view. In a typically flexible bungalow plan, a pocket door in each doorway into the dining room allowed it to be closed off from either or both adjacent areas. When open as shown, the free-flowing space allows vistas between rooms. As an alternative to the common use of box beams, both the living and dining room have a tray ceiling, entirely of plaster, which features a slightly recessed central panel.

125. **After:** Details of the living room, and of the adjacent entry and dining room, San Jose, California. Selected to work in harmony with each other, especially when viewed together through the open doorways, each space has been given its own decorative treatment. The dark woodwork is pleasingly combined with the various color schemes, each muted enough to blend without competing. In the foreground, the living room shows that light colors can work successfully with dark woodwork. The frieze has a widely spaced repeat of floral clusters using the stylized Glasgow rose associated with the work of Charles Rennie Mackintosh. The Glasgow rose became a favorite motif for textiles and art glass and was popular in America. Adapted from a fold-out insert, the pattern for the frieze was provided with a full-scale repeat in a supplement to Britain's *Journal of Decorative Art* dating around 1910. Geared toward the design and manufacturing trades of early twentieth-century England, this periodical often included inserts of new designs, intending them to be used by its subscribing artisans, designers, and architects. The geometric frieze seen in the dining room is reproduced in an original colorway from an actual sample in a 1915 pattern book distributed by the Remien & Kuhnert Company of Chicago. In a style popular in the Teens the frieze features a dropped pendant element as part of its repeat.

126. *Before:* Dining room in Berkeley, California. Viewed from the living room seen in figures 126 and 127, this dining room is entered through a wide pocket doorway directly opposite the fireplace. The original woodwork elements were intact, but the dining room's ceiling was faced with glued-on acoustical tiles. There are no box beams, and the frieze area of each wall is fully framed into long, separate panels. The kitchen, which also connects to the hallway off the living room, is reached through a swinging door just to the left of the sideboard.

127. *After:* Dining room in Berkeley, California. As in the living room, a deep green color scheme fuses the elements of this room into an overall harmony. Giving the room a stylish crown, bold repeats of a large-scale pendant frieze decorate the long horizontal panels. Its geometric linework and motif of highly stylized oak leaves are in a richly colored autumnal palette, colors recommended in the period as suitable for primary living spaces. The frieze was reproduced from remnants that were uncovered in a 1906 Los Angeles house in the West Adams district (fig. 44) beneath several layers of wallpaper. The design has since been found in a wallpaper catalog dating from the mid-Teens. Below it, a small geometric wallpaper pattern forms a simple background for period objects displayed on the plate rail. This pattern is also used to frame the perimeter of the ceiling. Its inside edges have been given interest by a crisply arranged framework of small borders, whose coloring and oak-leaf elements repeat from the frieze. A flourish of crossing lines at each corner creates a square, inspired by the corner detailing of many inlaid hardwood floors of the period (fig. 121). The Craftsman-style oak table and chairs are of the period, and the appliquéd and embroidered table linen has been reproduced from a period design. (For other views of this house see figs. 144, 145.)

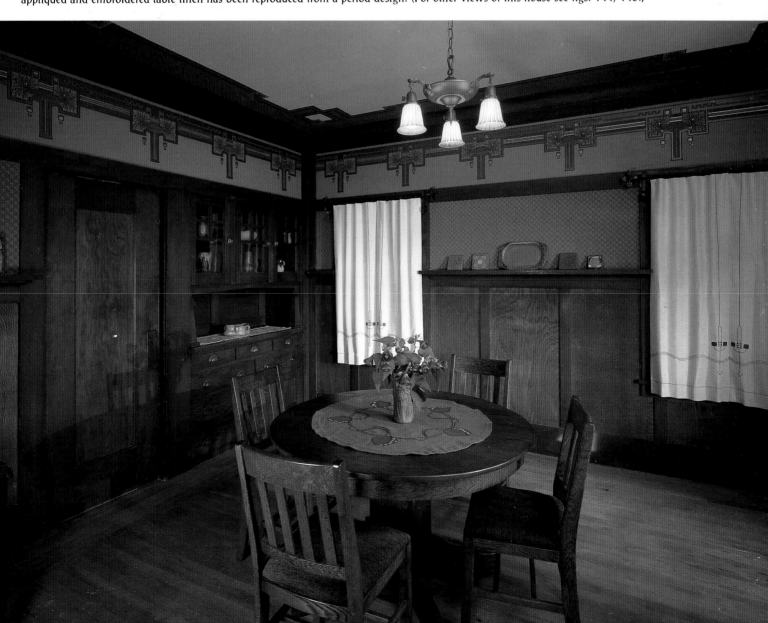

128. ***Before:*** Living room in Berkeley, California. As in a typical Craftsman bungalow, this living room is entered directly through its front door, from which this view was taken. Although it had managed to survive since the Teens with its fir woodwork unpainted, it was otherwise in a state of relatively benign neglect. Its painted walls were a rather dingy white. Fortunately, all of its characteristic woodwork elements were still intact. Box beams, dividing the ceiling into three well-proportioned panels, and a low wainscot, emphasizing the room's horizontal lines, gave the room some good basic bones. The original fireplace, and its attached built-ins, had also survived in decent condition. The windows were fitted with inappropriately large curtain rods and brackets. Visible through the doorway at right, a hallway leads to the bedrooms and bath. The black wrought-iron lighting fixtures, of a style especially popular in the Twenties, would look more at home in a Spanish Colonial Revival-style interior.

129. ***After:*** Living room in Berkeley, California. In the spirit of the ideal bungalow, this room now projects the warm and cozy atmosphere that invites gathering around its glowing fire. With the help of a wide-angle camera lens, more of its features, and pleasing proportions, are apparent. For a color scheme, the current owners selected a deep green, typical of the Arts and Crafts palette. This extensive use of green forges a harmonious complement to the reddish-orange highlights of the wood. The warm neutral color of the original matte-glazed tile facing of the fireplace and hearth wears its age well. The handprinted period-style wallpapers were adapted from a 1915 sample book, originally distributed by Remien & Kuhnert of Chicago. Their striking focal point, a geometric pendant frieze, features a stylized tree form. Its coloring includes rich shades of purple and gray-blue in a framework of deep green and accented by metallic gold. The wall areas are papered in an overall pattern of closely spaced leaves scattered with reflective bronze berries. Natural linen is used for the curtains, which are stenciled with a Glasgow rose motif. The room is furnished with period pieces of American Arts and Crafts oak furniture. Accessories of the period include assorted pieces of art pottery, a landscape painting, and the art-glass lamp on the table at the right. On the mantel are some handwoven baskets, hammered-copper vessels, and a framed watercolor. (For other views of this house see figs. 144, 145.)

130. **Before:** Living room in Los Angeles, California. An effect of snowblindness might well have been possible in this nearly colorless living room, where all the walls, woodwork, and even the brick fireplace had been covered with white paint. Only the stained accents of its leaded art-glass windows had survived the color purge. A classic 1909 bungalow of the West Adams district, the house is entered directly into the living room through its front door to the left. A squared column, on a low wall of built-ins, is visible at right. It forms part of a colonnade, the open division between the living and dining rooms that was popular in the period. Original built-ins were still in place on either side of the fireplace.

131. **After:** Living room in Los Angeles, California. The exhaustive efforts of the current owners to restore the living room's fir woodwork and brick fireplace to their original condition have been duly rewarded. Once again the room exudes the warmth and charm it was meant to have. The ceiling's box beams, not visible in figure 130, contribute to the strong lines of the room's woodwork. Framed by substantial capped casings that now have their proper visual weight, the art-glass panels sparkle with a new life. The characteristic pair of casement windows flanking the fireplace also have proper casings now. Punctuated by four square corbels, the mantel shelf aligns with the plate rail of the room's wood wainscot. The walls have been painted a soft cream to blend with the newly revealed limestone-colored brickwork of the fireplace. At the right, Roycroft collectibles are displayed on a built-in desk unit, which has drawers, cupboard space, and drop-down writing surface. The room is furnished with a mixture of period and newer Craftsman-style furnishings.

132. _Before:_ Dining room in Berkeley, California. Chiefly paneled by a high wood wainscot, a particularly strong feature of the dining room in this 1914 Craftsman-style house was its box-beam ceiling. Dividing the space into twelve panels of various sizes, it commanded attention, but floating above a broad, empty frieze area, it somehow seemed somewhat disconnected from the rest of the room. The original fir woodwork had remained unpainted. While the room was in good condition, it lacked color except for the wood. In lieu of a plate rail, the current owners had used the tiniest nails possible to secure a collection of Danish Christmas plates directly to the wood wainscot, but found their particular shade of blue difficult to incorporate into an appropriate color scheme. The room was also lacking a ceiling fixture. A pair of French doors, with narrow operable sidelight windows on either side, had recently been added by the current owners. Because there was never a built-in sideboard, a recessed window alcove provided a convenient place for a freestanding one. The house was designed by local architect Olin S. Grove as a speculative venture in the Northbrae area.

133. _After:_ Dining room in Berkeley, California. The room's surprising transformation occurred because of changes only to the area above its high wainscot. The frieze becomes alive with the rhythmic repeat and restrained color of a period-style pendant frieze. Of a design date close to that of the house, it seems to have an architectural presence that brings the ceiling beams into a close relation with the room below. The owners managed to find a suitable Craftsman-style ceiling fixture, whose design of squared brass tubing repeats the sturdy forms of the ceiling beams. In a glowingly stylish period treatment, light now reflects off the ceiling panels, or coffers, which have been covered with a gold paper whose delicate pattern suggests the effect of a gilded burlap. Continuing the colors of the frieze onto the ceiling, a narrow matching linear border outlines each panel and greatly enhances the presence of the box beams. To create a more spacious feeling, the rather massive furniture that was previously in the room was replaced by lighter-weight examples of the Craftsman style. A small-scale Gustav Stickley sideboard with tall legs and a built-in plate rack provides a bright and airy spot to display the period collectibles that have replaced the blue plates. This sideboard allows room for a pair of period side chairs to flank it and easier access to operate the casement windows. Because the room is also a circulation space to the kitchen and a den located to the left, the rounded form of the period oak dining table and chairs allows freer movement. The deep teal blue chair seats provide a color accent, and both color and pattern are introduced by the Oriental rugs on the original hardwood floors. In harmony with the Arts and Crafts style is a simple Japanese chest at the right, on which sits a period Sessions mantel clock.

134. *Before:* Dining room in Piedmont, California. This bungalow dining room of the Twenties showed an evolving Craftsman taste, but a major lack of color. Its current owners had already renovated less visible areas of the house, including a new kitchen, but design concepts were still under consideration for the main living spaces. This room's woodwork was intact. The owners had already stripped its walls of old wallpaper and refinished the woodwork. A memory of box beams lingers in the plaster ceiling, which is divided lengthwise by beam-like forms of a very shallow depth. A knee-high wainscot anchors the room. At the right, a built-in sideboard is of an important size. The popularity of French doors eventually eclipsed the use of pocket doors in the Twenties. This pair has unusual pointed glass divisions, which are also seen in the doors of the sideboard's china cabinet. Deciding against the Craftsman style for the dining room furnishings, they also added the gilded Twenties chandelier and purchased a simplified Baroque-inspired dining set of the same period.

135. *After:* Dining room in Piedmont, California. The walls of the dining room are given a lively prominence that mere paint couldn't muster. A striped wallpaper of soft olive green and kraft-paper brown etched with gold gives new elegance to the walls. In place of a frieze for the room's color and pattern accents, the shallow beam forms are trimmed with delicate, stencil-like borders in vivid colors. The neutral color and small scale of the geometric pattern on the beams are an effective foil for the narrow borders. Repeating in the low wainscot area, and restating the color of the wall's darker stripes, the same geometric pattern appears in olive green. The table's runner was reproduced from a design by Gustav Stickley. The strong red of the chairs, close to that of the pomegranates on the table, is echoed in the ceiling borders. Through the French doors, past the sponge-painted entry hall and the peaked doorway, is the living room. This bungalow has an unusual floor plan, that was probably designed specifically for this site. The result of an unusually long, narrow lot of very shallow depth, this view reveals the main living spaces aligned in a long vista, parallel to the street at left.

136. **Before:** Living room in Piedmont, California. Like the dining room of this house seen in figures 134 and 135, this living room had most of its original features, but color and pattern were conspicuously absent. The wall lights and ceiling fixtures were recently replaced by the current owners, and they are of a similar date and style as the ceiling fixture in the dining room. Starting in the far corner, a mantel shelf runs in a continuous sweep for about two-thirds the length of the room. Beneath it, to the right of the fireplace, there are a drop-front writing desk and built-in bookcases behind glass doors.

137. **After:** Living room in Piedmont, California. For the comfortable glow of this final scheme, the owners chose a subtle English wallpaper pattern called Marigold, reproduced from one originally designed in 1875 by William Morris. The early date of this pattern indicates that the beginnings of the Arts and Crafts Movement in England occurred during the Victorian era. However, many Morris patterns were produced as wallpapers and textiles throughout the years of the bungalow's popularity, and this living room shows that they continue to make ideal components for the American Arts and Crafts interior. The warm but neutral scheme of the wallpaper was selected for its compatibility with the colors of the woodwork and fireplace tiles and with the dining room. The long mantel shelf creates a generous display area for a collection of recent and period Arts and Crafts objects and artwork. The period-style mirror above the mantel was recently made. The Craftsman wall clock in the entry and the oak furniture is all of the period. The chairs in the living room feature recent Arts and Crafts textile designs on their pillows; the seat of the chair at right is covered with a Liberty fabric. The peaked form of the doorway and its squared columns standing at either side are highlighted against the entry hall's light sponge-painted finish.

138. **Before:** Den in Berkeley, California. In a misguided attempt to lighten up an otherwise all-wood original interior dating from 1905, the previous owners had slathered white paint on every inch of this den. The room was probably considered fair game, for it lacked the detailing and natural redwood walls and ceiling of the adjoining living and dining rooms. Because the den was completely white, it looked totally disembodied from not only the adjoining rooms but also the entire house. Inasmuch as it was so visible from the main living areas, the den clearly needed a design identity that would be compatible with the interior's original rustic character. Rather than perceive this as a limitation, the new owners became intrigued with the potential design freedom this room allowed them, and looked upon it as a blank canvas. Like the previous owners, they didn't feel compelled to consider making it an all-redwood room that duplicated the others, yet they realized that the restoration of the den would have to be carefully considered for its impact on the color and character of the adjoining spaces.

139. **After:** Den in Berkeley, California. Taking the plunge, the owners have given their den a completely new identity that is as inviting as the rest of their house. Convinced that the key to a successful solution lay in the use of rich natural color, the owners selected a palette of deep green and burnished metallics. This was also the scheme that proved to be the most compatible with the adjoining all-wood rooms. In a careful grouping of handprinted wallpapers that are reproduced from designs of the period, the room seems to have gained a true architectural presence. The striped pattern of the walls, highlighted with thin lines of dark metallic bronze, recalls the vertical rhythm of the board-and-batten paneling of the adjoining rooms. Previously lacking a defined frieze, the equal height of the spaces above the doors and windows provided a logical area. Because of its high visibility from adjacent spaces, the owners selected a 1911 English Arts and Crafts frieze design with a pine tree motif, a choice that was inspired by the rustic, woodsy character of the other rooms. The rustic theme is continued in a newly crafted ceiling fixture, which is decorated with sprigs of pine needles in the mica shade. The art-glass table lamp is also new. Additional Chraftsman-style furniture of the period has been obtained; also, the floral designs on the chair pillows and the pine cone motif of the curtains reproduce appropriate period designs. Using wallpaper or painted elements to suggest the scale of period architectural features is an economical way of doing so without using actual woodwork. (For other views of this house see figs. 30, 104.)

140. **Before:** Living room in Berkeley, California. This bright, cheerful living room is in a 1913 Northbrae area house that was designed by Bay area architect Charles Sumner Kaiser. The brightness was a quality that appealed to the new owners, and they wanted to preserve the feeling of the room. However, they knew that the white paint did little to enhance their collection of Arts and Crafts furnishings and objects. The room's woodwork, although original, was very simple, and there was no picture molding to define a frieze. While the fireplace was the room's focal point, it lacked emphasis, and the many windows needed appropriate coverings. The room was clearly ready for a revitalized design scheme.

141. **After:** Living room in Berkeley, California. With every bit of its cheer and light intact, the architecture of this living room has been balanced and integrated with its period furnishings by the introduction of soft-colored period wallpaper patterns in a creamy yellow. The upper walls have been given new emphasis by a pendant frieze, which has a motif of stylized oak leaves accented in a pale blue-gray. The paper on the walls has a subtly colored pattern of closely set leaves and berries. In this coloring, and from a distance, the pattern reads almost like an overall texture. Both frieze and wall patterns date from the mid-Teens. The pinkish brickwork and simple Craftsman-style wooden mantel incorporate a series of panels that effectively display a collection of period metalwork and art pottery. The smallest copper cup was recently crafted by one of the homeowners, who has a metalworking shop in the basement. Embroidered pillows, recreated to Arts and Crafts period styles, are used on the windowseat and the oak settle in the foreground. L. & J.G. Stickley made the settle and the Morris chair upholstered with leather at the right. The peacock pillow is from the Twenties. The matching slat-sided tabourets, at the center and in the far left corner, were made by Stickley Brothers. The round table, and the armchair with its original leather seat in the right foreground, are both by Gustav Stickley. On the round table is a period Dirk Van Erp lamp of hammered copper with a mica shade. Period Craftsman-style furnishings, whose manufacturers are unknown, include the tall clock and the rocking chair at the left. The handwoven wool Dhurrie rug, with deep green geometric linework, reproduces a design by Gustav Stickley. (For other views of this house see figs. 142, 143.)

142. *Before:* Dining room in Berkeley, California. When purchased by the current owners, the general condition of this dining room, like the living room, was in good condition and mostly intact. It was dominated by an original, richly colored wood wainscot that covered almost the full height of the wall, thus leaving an empty frieze space. The vertical board-and-batten detailing rose to a nicely flaring crown. Well proportioned, the room's buff-colored brick fireplace was simple, and had brick corbels under a wide mantel shelf. There were ample built-ins, including those to the right of the fireplace, and more beneath the window to the right. Somewhere along the way, the china cabinets had lost their glass doors. Most unusual was the wrought-iron chandelier, electrified at its center, but otherwise designed to hold candles. It had been custom made for the room in the 1970's by a Bay Area metalsmith named Carl Jennings. Although rather contemporary in design, the owners decided that the rough character of the ironwork made it compatible with the Arts and Crafts interior.

143. *After:* Dining room in Berkeley, California. Inasmuch as it has become a processional walkway for the strutting peacocks in the frieze, the high wainscot has an important new function. The wallpaper is based on an English pattern designed around the turn of the century by W. Dennington. The frieze was reproduced for this room by the use of an experimental computer-generated technique in which a color transparency of a full repeat of the design was scanned and finally laser-printed on paper in full color. This printing technique is a more refined version of the one used to make the large images in outdoor billboard advertisements. Two new wall lights with cylindrical mica shades that flank the windows were designed to coordinate with the iron chandelier. New glass doors in period style have been restored to the built-in china cabinets, and a growing collection of art pottery and ceramic tiles from the period are displayed around the room. The oak dining table and chairs were designed by Gustav Stickley and the chairs retain their original leather seats. On the hearth is an unusual English fire screen, possibly from the Twenties, on which the peacock is executed in painted and carved linoleum. (For other views of this house see figs. 140, 141.)

144. **Before:** Bedroom in Berkeley, California. The fact that its woodwork was all original did little to relieve the dinginess of this bungalow bedroom, which probably hadn't been repainted or papered in the last forty years. Its condition was similar to the rest of the house, but the new owners, undaunted, knew it had possibilities. Persuaded by the good light and air coming from a double window partly visible at right, they made this their bedroom. The poor condition of the wallpaper mural showing an Oriental pine tree, made them decide to remove it. However, the concept of an unusual wallpaper treatment for the room still appealed to them, for the new owners envisioned a solution more consistent with the Craftsman style of their house.

145. **After:** Bedroom in Berkeley, California. The bedroom of their dreams materialized more easily than the owners had imagined. Inspired by high-style examples of English and Scottish Arts and Crafts interiors, found in period design books and periodicals, the room's transformation was achieved with separate wallpaper elements. The handprinted papers were adapted and reproduced from period designs. Incorporating stylized bouquets of the Glasgow rose, a frieze of decorated panels was created above the picture molding. Similar bouquets of a larger scale are set near the tops of plain wall panels, and checkerboard borders are used to frame them. The strong architectural quality of the wall divisions gives the small space an elegance and presence that belie its size. Deceptively simple, the overall design evolved from the arrangement of the bed wall, which is logically divided into a large central panel flanked by two smaller ones. Echoing the vertical slats of the bed is the subtle striped pattern of the central panel. The side panels were repeated at the corners of the adjacent walls and suggest the effect of a bed alcove. As an important element of the room's decorative scheme, the Glasgow rose motif was stenciled on the custom-made bedspread, on the bed pillow, on the night-table cover, and as a border on the curtains. The flat-capped posts of the slatted oak bed and the use of shallow curves in the head- and footboards suggest the influence of English Arts and Crafts design. (For other views of this house see figs. 126–129.)

146. **Before:** Bedroom in San Francisco, California. Typical of many bedrooms in modern houses, this one characterizes the prevailing blandness of speculative building in a house dating to the early 1970s. Not exclusive to that decade, such standardization is common to many tract houses of the post-World War II era. In addition to the familiar shoddiness of hollow-core doors and minimal eight-foot ceilings, the baseboard and door casings were made with stock wood moldings of inconsequential width. Also, the horizontal sliding aluminum-framed window at right had no wood casings at all. The room was lit by a cheap, square glass fixture set close to the ceiling, a style widely used in bedrooms since the Fifties. The room's most redeeming feature was a walk-in closet. The realization that the basic proportions of this room were quite similar to those found in many bungalow bedrooms helped to establish a new design for the room.

147. **After:** Bedroom in San Francisco, California. Transformed into contemporary Arts and Crafts style, this room has also been inspired by Oriental design. With new woodwork trim throughout, the makeover was almost entirely achieved with standard moldings. Lending weight to the bottom of the walls is a new 6" high baseboard; all the other wood elements are made of plain 1" x 4" casing. Inspired by similar solutions seen in many bedrooms of Craftsman-style interiors, the door and window heights have been aligned with a continuous horizontal band of wood. The resulting frieze area has been left plain. The major architectural change was relocating the bathroom door, which now connects through the walk-in closet. The remaining door's proportions were enhanced by the addition of moldings at either side, which create tall flanking vertical panels topped by small square ones. This change has made the doorway appear wider, and gives it new importance. Replacing its closeable door is a hand-embroidered linen portière, recently adapted from a period design. The proportions of the window were similarly improved and integrated by new moldings. Recycled sliding Japanese shoji screens, backed with frosted glass, allow light to pass through their delicate wood patterns, but ensure privacy. They also conceal the unsightly aluminum window and outside security grille. Now painted the same color as the walls, the small framed panels could, if wanted, be dressed up with paint, stencils, fabric, or wallpaper. Eliminating the bathroom door has allowed room for a better placement of the bed. The recently crafted designs of the new bed and side table, which are handmade of cherry, are inspired by a fusion of Arts and Crafts and Oriental furniture traditions. A whimsical nineteenth-century touch is provided by the ebonized, folding rocking chair in the Anglo-Japanese style, associated with the Aesthetic Movement.

148. _Before:_ Bathroom in the Lanterman house, La Canada Flintridge, California. Unaltered since it was built in 1915, this bathroom reflects the remarkable state of preservation seen elsewhere in the Lanterman house, which was built as an oversized Craftsman-style bungalow with all the latest conveniences, and opened to the public as a house museum in 1993. Occasional faint traces of plants are visible under the grime above the high tile wainscot. The massive pedestal tub is fitted with centrally mounted plumbing hardware. It also retains its original shower fittings with a large shower head ringed by a circular curtain rod. All of the room's hardware still has its original nickel-plated finish. The handsome pedestal sink, with a base in the form of a fluted classical column, has "mixer" faucet fittings that blend the hot and cold water, a convenience now taken for granted, but which was an upgrade at the time. At left, a pair of leather strops still hang ready to sharpen razors for shaving. The toilet, with its tank mounted on the wall, is typical of the period. Above it, the pair of handles suspended on chains open or close a ventilation hatch in the ceiling. The lower walls are surfaced in a white-tile wainscot; the 3" x 6" glazed tiles were considered the hygienic standard of the day.

149. _After:_ Bathroom in the Lanterman house, La Canada Flintridge, California. The restored condition of this bathroom is testimony to what a difference a good cleaning can make. Previously all but invisible, the decorative groups of iris on the upper walls have been beautifully revealed again thanks to the cleaning and restoration by Pinson and Ware. A few other minor adjustments were also made. An unsightly grab bar was removed from above the tub, the woodwork was repainted to freshen its original color, and a dirty and unnecessary roller blind was removed from the window, revealing a glimpse of greenery above lower panels of original frosted glass. (For other views of this house see fig. 81 and figs. 128–131 in _The Bungalow_.)

150. **Before:** Bathroom in Santa Cruz, California. Somewhere along the way, this bungalow's bathroom was led astray. Its changes had come out of good intentions, but were in decided conflict with the spirit and date of the house, which was built in the Teens. Whoever remodeled this bathroom must have had some respect for the past, for they kept the original built-in medicine cabinet with its beveled-glass mirrored door, as well as one of the two small double-hung windows that flanked it. But, all of the original plumbing fixtures and hardware had been replaced. A boxy built-in sink cabinet was installed, which provided some storage but made the room feel rather cramped. When this view was taken, the current owners were just about to dismantle the room. Visible in the foreground, across the lower right corner, is part of a built-in plywood cabinet which had been dislodged from the wall prior to its removal. Like the sink cabinet, it had been added to provide storage, but so overwhelmed the small room that it became claustrophobic.

151. **After:** Bathroom in Santa Cruz, California. In recreating a period bathroom design, the owner's goal to put back only what had probably been there originally has been admirably achieved. Even if it hadn't been obvious that one of the small windows had been covered over to incorporate shower plumbing, there was compelling structural evidence of it once the wall was opened up. With its pair of windows restored, the intended natural lighting around the medicine cabinet has also returned. It was determined that the height of the original wainscot area originally aligned with the wood casing below the windows. It has been newly refaced with traditional 3" x 6" white glazed ceramic tiles set with narrow grout lines, which was common in many bungalow bathrooms. The use of a wood baseboard and wood molding above to cap the tile was a viable alternative to the expense of costly ceramic trim pieces. The flooring is a reissued version of the small hexagonal white tiles that were a widely used standard finish of the period. A new pedestal sink with classic styling allows the feeling of space and ease of cleaning to return to the area below the windows. A new toilet that matches the sink is at lower left. A period claw-foot tub was reconditioned and fitted with free-standing shower hardware and an enclosing curtain rod attached to the ceiling. The owner's concession to personal taste was to add some color to a room that most likely would originally have been all white. The sides and feet of the tub have been painted a deep blue, and a grayish lavender-blue was used on the woodwork—an effective background for the bright salmon towels.

Inside
Greene and Greene
INTERIORS FROM THE
THORSEN AND GAMBLE HOUSES

The work of the American architects Charles Sumner Greene (1868–1957) and Henry Mather Greene (1870–1954), two brothers whose architectural partnership in Pasadena, California, was known as Greene and Greene, is almost inseparable from any discussion of Arts and Crafts architecture or interiors in this country. While their domestic commissions were relatively few and span only a very short period of time, their resulting stature has become legendary. Following the lead of architectural historians Robert Judson Clark and Randell Makinson, the term "ultimate bungalows" has been used to describe some of the Greenes' most notable commissions. Collectively, these houses are considered the artistic peak of their collaboration. Included among them are the Robert R. Blacker House (1907–1908) and the David B. Gamble House (1907–1909) in Pasadena; the Charles M. Pratt House (1908–1909) in Ojai, California; and the William R. Thorsen House in Berkeley, California (1908–1910).

Not intended to be taken literally, the "ultimate bungalow" sobriquet refers essentially to the harmonious relationship shared by these houses to their respective sites, and the skillful, integrated use of natural materials and revealed construction in their design. The parallels between these larger, more sumptuous houses and their modest bungalow counterparts of the same period seemed to invite the comparison; the Greenes' work, while using a vocabulary of details unique to them, is also derived from sources of inspiration common to the Craftsman style. A strong, clear sense of structure underlies their designs and is one source of the great beauty of the houses they built.

The designs of these houses seemed to grow from a fertile combination of client needs, mutual confidence, practical requirements of their building sites, and local climatic conditions. The houses are inextricably linked to their sites by a horizontal emphasis that has been com-

pared to that of the Prairie style, which was concurrently active in the Midwest. However, the Greenes' houses relate differently to the land than Prairie houses, for their houses are essentially celebrations of wood: its structural capabilities, its sense of joinery, and its richly varied textures and colors. They took obvious delight in using wood to express their creative ideas—from the overall forms of the houses to the renowned finishes and furnishings created for their interiors.

Traditionally trained architects, the Greenes had studied at the Massachusetts Institute of Technology and briefly lived and worked in the Boston area before deciding to migrate west. For reasons of health, their parents had already relocated in Pasadena and encouraged their sons to join them. That city was evolving from its beginnings as a winter resort and retirement mecca to a choice residential area for some of America's wealthiest families. The opportunities for new work there and elsewhere in Southern California looked promising. While on their way west, the Greenes stopped in Chicago to attend the World's Columbian Exposition of 1893. Most of the Exposition's architecture was dominated by Beaux Arts classicism, which earned the event its nickname of the "White City." It was the prevalence of this style throughout the country that progressive architects, such as Louis Sullivan and Frank Lloyd Wright, were opposed to. Sullivan's distinctively original Transportation Building at the Exposition struck a lone chord among the event's other major buildings. Rather than be trapped creatively by the rigid vocabulary of historicism, Sullivan and Wright sought to establish a more organic American approach to new architecture. For greater public understanding and acceptance, such thinking would have to wait another generation for the arrival of modernism. For the Greenes, however, the examples of authentic Japanese architecture to be seen

152. The front of the Thorsen House, Berkeley, California. The outside corner of the dark-shingled building is dominated at the left by a clinker-brick chimney, and the large bay window of the dining room. The foundation level is also faced with the same textured brick. The projecting roof of the bay window forms an open terrace for a guest bedroom above it. Entry to the front of the house from the street is through either of two lantern-hung gateways, each leading to a pair of clinker-brick stairways that mount to the entry portico. Out of view at the left, the side elevation rises with the hill, an additional partial story contained in a side-facing gable, and terminates in a large garage connected by an open-air breezeway.

153. The front door of the Thorsen House. Highlighted by the dark shingles, the handsome front door, transom, and adjacent side window of light-colored Burma teak frame panels of art glass, each of which has part of a stylized tree design that arches across all of them. The distinctive earthenware garden pots were designed by the Greenes and manufactured by Gladding McBean. They are identical to those made for the Gamble House, and were probably made at the same time. Both were speckled with a black glaze that was lightly flicked on to create texture. Their trademark rounded beam ends and rafter-tails are also visible under the portico roof. Similar to other outdoor areas of the house, the floor of the entry terrace is bordered by brick and inset with plain terra-cotta tiles.

154. The entry hall, looking toward the front door of the Thorsen House. This elegant entry hall combines Burma teak paneling with sumptuous art glass having a tree motif. The original art-glass lantern, suspended from leather straps, is repeated in other areas of the entry hall, and was a form of lighting favored by the Greenes. To the left of the front door, a built-in mirror and coat hooks are provided between vertical battens. At the top of the wainscot, the lengths of wood have been artfully linked by scarf-joints, a favorite device of the architects that reappears elsewhere in this house and in other projects. Another favorite detail is the small, square ebony pegs that stud the woodwork. They are shallow plugs that cover the countersunk brass screws. The diagonally laid oak flooring makes the hall feel wider and adds movement to the area. The wide doorway at the left leads to the living room and is fitted with French doors. Opposite the front door, French doors lead to an outdoor terrace and to views of the garden. Chinese antiques placed here for the exhibition include a nineteenth-century bench at the right, and an eighteenth-century side table at the left, on which is seen a green vase by Paul Revere Pottery/Saturday Evening Girls.

at this international event were more intriguing and eventually inspiring. It took several years before this experience had a recognizable influence on their work.

From the beginning of their careers, the Greenes preferred residential work as the vehicle of expression for their creative energies. Their early architectural work, reflecting mainstream public taste, was influenced by the Queen Anne, Mission, and Colonial Revival styles. While their most frequently cited design influence is the Japanese, their decorative work for interiors was particularly affected by the richness of Chinese design. Although a strong Oriental influence characterizes their most famous projects, they brought to each commission a personal interpretation that was far from literal, but unique, and completely American.

The David B. Gamble House in Pasadena is their most famous work, and it survives in splendidly original condition. One of the most treasured icons of the American Arts and Crafts Movement, it is widely admired for the beauty and harmony of its structure and contents. Since 1966, when it was given to the city of Pasadena by the Gamble family, the Gamble House has been open to the public. In a joint agreement with the University of Southern California, it is administered by their School of Architecture as a house museum, and due to this accessibility by the public it continues to embody and illuminate the American Arts and Crafts Movement for countless students and visitors.

Ironically, the renown of the Gamble House has eclipsed much of the attention due the other "ultimate bungalows." Unfortunately, they are not open to the public, and none has retained the completeness of its original furnishings like the Gamble House.

The William K. Thorsen House is one of the Northern California examples of the Greenes' work. The last (but not the least) of the "ultimate bungalow" group, it is far removed from the atmospheric Southern California landscape and climate most associated with their work. Since 1943, the Thorsen House, which is close to the University of California's Berkeley campus, has been home to a college fraternity, the Alpha of California chapter of the Sigma Phi Society. Very fortunately, through the years, the resident members of the fraternity, many students of architecture among them, have taken great pride in their building. Its most significant main living spaces have survived remarkably well and remain in nearly original condition. Edward R. Bosley, who has been the director of the Gamble House since 1992, lived in the Thorsen House in the 1970s as a member of the Sigma Phi Society. His interest in its architecture and in the work of Greene and Greene took root during that period. While still attending college, he helped to get the house placed on the National Register of Historic Places in 1978.

The photographs of the Thorsen House that follow were taken when it was set up for a unique exhibition, "Last of the Ultimate Bungalows: The William R. Thorsen House of Greene and Greene," which had a two-month run in the summer of 1996. It was presented by The Gamble House/ University of Southern California, in cooperation with the College of Environmental Design Documents Collection of the University of California, Berkeley, the California Sigma Phi Alumni Association, and the Sigma Phi Society, Alpha of California active chapter. For the first time in more than half a century, the original handcrafted furnishings designed by the architects were reunited with the house. Exhibition designer James M. Marrin worked with period photographs of the interiors, and not only was the Thorsens' furniture accurately arranged, but also it was placed on their original Oriental carpets. Staged as a dual benefit, revenues from the event helped to launch the funding campaign for seismic upgrading at the Thorsen House and for ongoing maintenance expenses at the Gamble House.

Such an exhibition had been a long-time goal of Edward Bosley's, ever since he had learned that the original Thorsen furniture was still together and in private hands. Fortunately, in 1990, the Gamble House was the recipient of an anonymous bequest of all the Thorsen furniture designed by the Greenes, along with the Thorsens' original Oriental carpets. Since the Gamble House was already full of its own furnishings, the permanent home of this bequest became the Virginia Steele Scott Gallery at the Huntington Library and Art Collection in nearby San Marino, California.

The exhibition was co-curated by a trio of Greene and Greene scholars: Edward Bosley, Robert Judson Clark, and Randell L. Makinson. Robert Judson Clark taught at Princeton University between 1968 and 1996 as a professor in the Department of Art and Archeology, and is also well known for his involvement in the groundbreaking exhibition at Princeton in 1972, "The Arts and Crafts Movement in America 1876–1916." Makinson, a restoration architect, has authored two landmark books, *Greene and Greene: Architecture as Fine Art*, published in 1977, and *Greene and Greene: Furniture and Related Designs*, published in 1979. He was also the former director of the Gamble House for a twenty-six-year period, prior to Bosley's appointment. Like Bosley, both Clark and Makinson, early in their careers, had become familiar with the significance of the Thorsen House, while pursuing independent research and study of Greene and Greene.

Built for lumberman William Randolph Thorsen and his wife, Caroline Canfield Thorsen, the house is on a compact urban site. Placed on a corner, it is set fairly close to the street on two sides, and there is a peaceful enclosed garden behind its shingled L-shape form. The building

exudes a feeling of dignity and refinement, yet celebrates its wooden structure, with the Greenes' trademark round-edge beams and rafter-tails projecting from beneath the eaves of its sloping roof. Because of differences in climate, this house shows that some of its features have been modified from what the Greenes did in Southern California. The cooler and foggier environment of Berkeley made it necessary for the roof overhangs to be made shallower to allow more light to enter the interior. The window areas of the main living spaces are also unusually large and relatively unshaded. Most of the outdoor living areas are also more sheltered, although still designed to take advantage of a rather mild climate. There is an extensive use of clinker brick at the foundation level, helping to tie the structure to its slightly sloping site. Both outside and inside, the Greenes incorporated visual references to Mr. Thorsen's nautical interests and possibly his Scandinavian heritage. Stylized Viking ships appear as motifs on the metalwork of the front gates at the sidewalk level, and in the living room the form of a distinctively pointed bay window has been likened to a ship's prow.

The Thorsens had some connections with other "ultimate bungalow" owners, which suggests that client referrals were a good source of commissions for the Greenes. Caroline Thorsen had been a Vassar College roommate of Mrs. Pratt. She was also the sister of Mrs. Blacker, whose house she apparently admired enough to want something similar for her own family. Although the Thorsens were not directly linked to the Gambles, the fact that the Greenes had also designed a similar house for them was certainly significant common ground. It is important to realize that the informality and ease that characterized the Greenes' commodious wooden houses were not qualities typically associated with homes of wealthy people. Most of the homes built by the very rich in America were created in the styles of English country houses, Italian villas, or French châteaux, in order to impress their peers as well as to inflate their own sense of status.

155. (Opposite) A portion of the living room seen from the entry hall of the Thorsen House. Upon entering the room, a sweeping wall of built-in cabinetry is immediately visible at the left. It includes a commodious drop-front desk with pigeonholes and small drawers below a pair of open display shelves. Honduras mahogany is used throughout the room. Of the things on display, only the framed photograph of the Blacker House, on the shelf above the desk, belonged to the Thorsens. The other objects include copper pieces by Dirk Van Erp; a Tiffany bronze and glass lamp and matching picture frame next to a green Arequipa vase; two small Grueby matte-green vases; and a plate by Pewabic Pottery at the left above. Distinctive woodwork, whose form implies structure, defines the perimeter of the ceiling, and a narrow frieze area is accented with delicate hand-painting. Surprisingly, the Thorsens' living room was not originally specified to contain Greene and Greene pieces. For the exhibition, one of their superb dining-room side chairs with its original leather seat was placed by the desk. An eighteenth-century Chinese armchair is nearby at the right. Visible above the fireplace mantel, beyond the glass-fronted bookcase, is another display shelf. Original ebony and art-glass wall lights hang on either side of the mantel. For the ceiling, the architects designed an early form of recessed lighting: back-lit, flush-mounted art-glass panels outlined with flat wood moldings. These are a handsome and unusual alternative to hanging fixtures, and were a progressive solution for the period. Appearing somewhat flattened out, only one side of a room-wide, "ship's prow" bay window is visible at the far end of the room. The distinctive silhouette of its glazing bar shows through the curtains. In front of it on an antique Chinese table is a Tiffany turtle-back lamp of bronze and iridescent glass, which was kept by the Thorsens in this room. There is a large Grueby matte-green floor vase at the left of the window.

(Overleaf) 156. The living room, looking toward the fireplace and entry hall of the Thorsen House. The living room is probably the most beautiful room in the house. In the far corner the wide doorway to the entry hall reveals a distant view to the foot of the staircase. The two recessed lighting fixtures are visible in the ceiling. The Greenes originally planned to include a central hanging fixture in this room, but it was never executed, and a small round cedar panel covers its unused wiring. The great focal point of the room is its exceptionally wide fireplace emphasized by the polished steel frame of the fireplace opening. A softly mottled Grueby-tile facing extends onto the hearth, and the tile is inlaid with accents of tiny contrasting ceramic chips. A low "fire bench," also designed by the Greenes, provides a place to sit at the hearth. Several glass-fronted bookcases are built into the fireplace wall, and more are out of view on the opposing wall. Dividing the frieze at regular intervals, sprays of handpainted branches, which radiate from U-shaped woodwork elements, are set below scarf-joints in the lengths of wood near the ceiling. In 1913, after the house was completed, the library table with an oval top decorated with inlaid designs was made for this room. Although Charles was responsible for designing most of the Greenes' furniture, this piece has been attributed to Henry Greene. The lamp on the table is a reproduction in the style of Louis Comfort Tiffany. The remaining furniture on view are antique Chinese pieces placed here for the exhibition. The Oriental rugs are from the Thorsens' collection.

157. Detail of fireplace mantel and frieze in the living room of the Thorsen House. Showing the beauty and refinement that the Greenes accomplished in their interiors, this junction of fireplace mantel, built-in bookcase, and frieze has a harmonious complexity. Some of the delicate inlaid chips of the fireplace's Grueby-tile facing are visible at the left and center. One of a pair, the backplate and pierced framework of the art-glass wall light are made of ebony. Note again the square ebony pegs used to cover screw holes in the Honduras mahogany. The handpainted flowering branches that spring from the vase-like woodwork element is attributed to Charles Greene. The shelf above the mantel provides handsome display space for typical decorative objects of the Craftsman period. The curtained window at the right overlooks the rear garden.

158. Den of the Thorsen House. This room is located directly off the entry hall opposite the foot of the staircase. For the exhibition, the wall panels, originally inset with fabric, were re-covered in a natural linen by student residents. Vertical wood elements that create panels in the wall and support display shelves at the corners are connected by a horizontal molding that aligns with the curtain valance. The handcrafted copper ceiling fixture casts a soft glow of indirect light onto the ceiling, and was reproduced from the Greenes' design for the original one. For the exhibition, the den was set up with Arts and Crafts furnishings designed by others. Oak furniture by Gustav Stickley includes the round lamp table and rocking chair at right and the large leather-cushioned oak settle at left, on which is a pillow made from a small Chinese rug. The copper lamp with the mica shade is fueled with kerosene and was made by Dirk Van Erp about 1910. He also made the copper vase on the shelf at the right and the jardinière on the small L. & J.G. Stickley stand in front of the window. On the shelf at the left is a green vase painted with a blue iris design made by Paul Revere Pottery/Saturday Evening Girls around 1912. The triptych above the settle was done by Marian Holden Pope in 1902 as a study for an allegorical mural in the Oakland Carnegie Library.

159. Dining room of the Thorsen House. A masterpiece of integrated design by Greene and Greene, the dining room is shown furnished exactly as it was when the Thorsens lived here. Each element in the Honduras mahogany-paneled room combines the architects' elegant sense of design with the exceptionally high level of craftsmanship they demanded for their clients. In the dining table, on which is a Fulper Pottery bowl, and chairs ebony pegs and inlay are highlighted against the mahogany, in what are considered to be among the best of Charles Greene's designs. Using insets of oak, fruitwood, and abalone shell, each piece features delicate inlaid motifs of flowering vinca, which also occur across the crest rail of each dining chair. The fireplace at left has a facing of Rookwood Pottery tile which is inlaid with tiny reflective ceramic chips that are set in a meandering pattern. The room's rectangular wall lights have a mahogany framework and art-glass shades. Complementing them are the shallow, box-like forms of the wood and art-glass ceiling fixtures with flush-mounted backplates. The ceiling fixtures are placed so they are centered over the dining table when it is extended to seat fourteen. At the far wall, a built-in china cabinet with art-glass doors is located over a freestanding serving table displaying two Fulper Pottery pieces. The door with the backlit glass panels at the left leads to a large serving pantry connected to the kitchen. The wide doorway opens to one end of the entry hall. The single doorways across the hall, each having a portière, lead to a hall closet at the left, and to the kitchen at the right.

160. Detail of the dining room fireplace at the Thorsen House. The quality and refinement inherent in the Greenes' architectural detailing is on a par with that of their celebrated furniture. This detail shows the intricate technique required to inlay tiny contrasting ceramic chips into the Rookwood-tile facing of the fireplace. To create the meandering design it was necessary to cut the curving elements into plain background tile, and then each chip was placed with the exacting skill of an artist's brushstroke. Here again is a close look at the Greenes' famous woodwork, with luminous Honduras mahogany shaped with rounded edges and studded with their signature square pegs of ebony.

161. Detail of the dining-room frieze at the Thorsen House. Seen here is the handpainted decoration that accents each corner of the frieze area, and as in the living room, the painting has been attributed to Charles Greene. It features a grapevine motif, which was considered appropriate for dining rooms during the period. The arrangement of vines and grape clusters are set against what appear to be cut-out wood panels. Painted on canvas over plaster, the texture of the material is visible on the ochre-colored ceiling that has darkened with age.

162. Detail of the entry-hall ceiling in the Thorsen House. Where the staircase begins its rise, the wood moldings that define the frieze interact at an outside corner. In this area the square pegs are of the same Burma teak as the woodwork and paneling. As the wall turns the corner, a lap-joint is highlighted, and the wall at left shows the transition to an all-wood frieze area. The subtle texture of the painted, canvas-lined frieze area and matching ceiling is more apparent at this close range.

163. (Opposite) Staircase in the entry hall of the Thorsen House. A distinctively inlaid newel post with peg-like ebony forms of differing sizes arranged in an irregular vertical rhythm anchors the foot of the staircase. Sleek, generous slabs of softly rounded Burma teak are used to create the railing, which is substantial, but elegantly detailed. In a masterful activation of negative space between the horizontal teak railing elements, the Greenes incorporated the subtle linear movement of the cloud lift. Occurring on both edges of the wood slab held between them, the lower edge of the top rail and the top of the stairway's stringer mirror the same cloud-lift form. To minimize interruption of the railing's sweep, paired vertical supports are placed at rather wide intervals. The lamp on the table at the left was designed by Greene and Greene for the 1904 Adelaide Tichenor House in Long Beach, California, which was the first of their commissions to include the design of coordinating furniture. Combining a mica-backed shade of pierced bronze with a ship and wave motif over a Chinese ceramic base, the lamp seems to anticipate the nautical references used in the Thorsen House. It rests on an eighteenth-century Chinese table made of cypress. At right, a large window high on the wall, which provides views of the garden, also admits light into the first floor. A large framed photograph above the wainscot at the landing shows the Thorsen House during construction. To the right, a small teak table was designed by the Greenes, and on it sits a matte-green Grueby vase.

Combining influences of Oriental, Craftsman, and English Arts and Crafts design, the Greenes fashioned their houses and furnishings into harmonious and artistic ensembles of extraordinary workmanship. The Greenes were fortunate in having superb craftspeople to bring their designs to life. Swedish woodworkers and brothers Peter and John Hall brought traditions of their native country and a staff of Scandinavian craftspeople with them. They set up shop in Pasadena to produce work for the Greenes' increasingly complex commissions, and were extensively involved in the building construction and production of furniture for the Blacker, Gamble, Pratt, and Thorsen houses. One of their skilled employees, William Isaac Ott (along with his entire family), was sent to Berkeley to supervise the construction of the Thorsen House. Another employee of the Halls, a Scandinavian craftsman named Jack Petersen, was responsible for building the Thorsen House furniture, which was made on site in a temporary workshop set up in the basement. The pieces designed and made for the Thorsen House are considered to be some of Greene and Greene's finest work. While Charles Greene is credited with most of the firm's furniture designs, Henry Greene was also a very capable designer.

Although they probably would have preferred it that way, not every piece of furniture originally in the Thorsen House was designed or approved by the Greenes. Like

164. Detail of the staircase railing in the Thorsen House. Most apparent at the turn of the stair landing, the smoothly sculptural quality of the staircase forms was made to be touched. Simple, staggered forms rise in a graceful transition between two adjacent squared newel posts. Washed with natural light from the stairwell window, the richness of the teak's color, graining pattern, and texture is highlighted. In a handsome and sturdy detail that occurs elsewhere in pairs, the pegged vertical support at the left is made of two separate pieces. Sandwiched together, they are carefully fitted into the intersecting horizontal railing elements and provide the structural support needed for the massive railing design.

many other homeowners, the Thorsens had rather eclectic tastes in furniture, and also enjoyed mixing styles and periods. Collectors of American antiques, they even owned some reproductions of antiques in the Colonial Revival style. For the recent exhibition it was necessary to eliminate this part of the original furnishings, for the specific focus was to interpret the designs of Greene and Greene. Nevertheless, to help enhance the room settings some other sympathetic furnishings and decorative objects were brought in. Not original to the house, some examples of antique Chinese furniture were placed in the entry hall and living room. The architects were known to have admired and specified Gustav Stickley furniture for other projects, and some of his pieces were also included to help refurnish the den and an upstairs guest room.

The purpose of these photographs is to provide the feeling of moving sequentially through an entire Greene and Greene interior. Because we could not photograph every part of the Thorsen House, the exterior and primary first-floor living spaces are most fully represented, and some details of Mrs. Thorsen's bedroom are shown. We also decided that the Greenes' handling of private and utility spaces could be represented by a comparable house. For that reason, some rooms and details of the Gamble House have also been included here. (For other views of the Gamble House see figs. 123–127 in *The Bungalow*.)

165. Detail of the fireplace in Mrs. Thorsen's bedroom. Characteristic of the Port Orford cedar woodwork seen in adjoining areas of the second floor, this fireplace shows the elegance that is exemplified in the whole house. Set against painted walls of olive-green, its design employs fewer pegs and less layered complexity. Providing a feeling of softness, the rounded, cascading forms of a corbeled bracket support the mantel. The lap-joint of the mantel's outside corner is repeated throughout the house. The creamy yellow Rookwood-tile facing has small clusters of inlaid ceramic bits, which accent its intersecting grout lines. Part of a master-suite arrangement, this room is significantly larger than Mr. Thorsen's adjoining bedroom.

166. Detail of a doorway and wall light in Mrs. Thorsen's bedroom. Of a form that echoes those of the fireplace mantel, a pegged corbeled bracket is speared by a wooden dowel. The dowel was intended to support a portière, and the doorway opening is fitted with a single-width pocket door, to avoid interference with the fabric. With its rounded backplate carefully notched into the flat molding above it, a single wall light of simple form hangs to one side of the doorway that leads to Mr. Thorsen's bedroom.

167. Master bedroom of the Gamble House, Pasadena, California. Spacious and elegant, the Gambles' master bedroom is finished in Port Orford cedar, and it is entered from a spacious second-floor stair hall through the door at the right. An entry alcove is formed by a deep walk-in closet at the right and the row of built-in wardrobe cabinets at the left. These have tall wooden handles that are cleverly designed both to conceal and operate their latch mechanisms. They unlatch when they are twisted sideways. A separate storage drawer, placed at floor level, is under each door. The room is indirectly lit by unusual light fixtures of cedar that are suspended from leather straps and decorated with inlays of abalone shell. The various textiles used in this room are not original. Separated by a structural beam, the roomy inglenook at the left was arranged to maximize its visibility and use. The fireplace is faced with rectangular tiles, the earthy color of which harmonizes with that of the surrounding cedar. Blue and brown ceramic tiles are used to create the series of small accent panels. The andirons were designed by the Greenes. They are made of cast and polished steel with some welded decoration. At either side of the cedar panel above the mantel there is carved, low-relief decoration in an abstract linear motif. The other fixed elements of the inglenook are asymmetrically placed and include the deep built-in bench at right, the base of which incorporates a heating vent at the front end. Above the bench an interior casement window with art-glass panels opens for added air circulation above the main stairwell (fig. 168). Next to it, open shelves have a display of small decorative objects. Mounted above the bench is a built-in wall light with an elongated wooden backplate of stepped form. This room's exceptional matching suite of freestanding furniture is made of black walnut and has delicate floral inlays of fruitwoods and bits of semiprecious stones, including lapis lazuli and turquoise. The range of furniture includes the pair of rocking chairs at the left, each with a rounded cut-out in the shape of a Japanese tsuba (or sword guard) near the top of its flaring backsplat. In the foreground, similar cut-out shapes are seen at the center of the footboard of each bed. Other matching pieces, not in view, include a nightstand; a bureau and a taller chiffonier; a drop-front writing desk and chair, and two other other side chairs and a "shoe chair." To the left of the inglenook, a door leads to an adjoining master bath, and another door leads to one of three large open-air sleeping porches that the Greenes incorporated into the house.

168. Detail of the interior window above the main stairwell of the Gamble House. Allowing a glimpse into the master bedroom from the second floor stairhall, this casement window with striking leaded art-glass panels opens to provide additional air circulation. Situated above the nightstand between the two beds, a single bedroom wall light is visible through the window. With oversized lap-joint detailing, the top of the window's projecting wood casing is aligned with the molding that continues around the stairhall below the frieze area. A large bronze and art-glass lantern with a gracefully curving top is suspended below the window, and it illuminates the staircase below.

169. Detail of the fireplace in Aunt Julia's bedroom in the Gamble House. Mrs. Gamble's sister, Julia Huggins, was a close family member and a permanent resident of the house. As part of their original design her own requirements were carefully considered and implemented by the Greenes. In order to display a group of small collectibles, a pair of built-in display cupboards were fitted with simple leaded-glass doors at either side of the mantel shelf. The corbeled form of the pegged bracket below the cabinet, and the creamy yellow Rookwood-tile facing, are both similar to the design used for Mrs. Thorsen's bedroom fireplace (fig. 165). At the right of the fireplace one of four wooden doors conceals extensive built-in drawer and wardrobe storage. A door to the second floor stairhall is just to the left of the fireplace, and another closet is situated next to that door. French doors lead from this bedroom to a large open-air sleeping porch that is also connected to one end of the second-floor stairhall. A suite of ash and rattan furniture was designed for the room. Both wood and rattan were colored with the same stain, creating a subtle color harmony between them. A stain was also applied to the room's Port Orford cedar woodwork.

170. Guest bedroom at the Gamble House. This bedroom is located off a small vestibule that adjoins the main entry hall, so as to enable houseguests to be separate from the family bedrooms upstairs. It is self-contained and has a separate adjoining bathroom. The room is lit by superb mahogany and art-glass wall fixtures of a finer quality than any in the other bedrooms. Suspended from projecting wood brackets by metal straps, their elongated wooden backplates are detailed with delicate silver-wire inlay. The pair of nickel-plated brass beds reveal the hand of the Greenes in their carefully proportioned and rounded forms, and vertical elements of the bed frames have some incised decoration. Their use of cascading forms in a silvery finish anticipates Art Deco and Moderne designs by two or three decades. The maple furniture made for this room is embellished with silver-wire inlays combined with Indonesian vermillion wood. The desk standing between the windows has a separate "writing box" placed on it, which allowed guests to move it around the house during their stay. Both the writing desk and the bureau (out of view) have sterling silver handles on the drawers. The triple-casement window on the far wall shows the distinctive shape of the glazing bar that is repeated on many windows throughout the house.

171. Detail of a wall light in Aunt Julia's bedroom at the Gamble House. Typical of the wall lights often used by the Greenes, this fixture hangs at the left of the French doors leading to the sleeping porch. A portion of the casing for the French doors is visible at the right. The fixture's rounded backplate shows the Greenes' screw-hiding pegs and the projecting wood support for the hanging light. This fixture is quite similar to the wall light in Mrs. Thorsen's bedroom.

172. Detail of a bathroom in the Gamble House. Although this bathroom is the one used by Aunt Julia Huggins, it is typical of the others in the house. It is also quite similar to bathrooms in much more modest houses. All of the wood-work has been painted white, and the lower walls are finished with a wainscot of the popular white, high-gloss glazed ceramic tile. The floors, not visible here, are laid with a larger version of the unglazed white hexagonal tiles that were universally popular at the time. A plain, painted wood molding terminates the tile wainscot in a line that continues across the top of the casement windows. A pair of painted wood wall lights, with rounded rectangular backplates, are inset with pegged accents of unpainted oak. A mirrored medicine cabinet is framed with round-edge moldings with crossed corners, also pegged with oak. This was designed as a "split bath," for the toilet is located in a separate com-partment with a door that opens into the hallway.

173. The kitchen in the Gamble House. The Gamble household was, of course, one that employed servants, and their needs seem to have been as carefully considered by the architects as those of the Gamble family members. The kitchen has a cheerful and airy quality that must have been uplifting for those who worked in it. The large work table and all of the flooring and built-in wall of drawers, storage cupboards, and glass-fronted china cabinets are made of maple. The extensive countertop is sugar pine. To the left, a doorway leads to the servants' stairs and to the hall area across from the dining room. The butler's pantry is located even further to the left and opens into the dining room. It has generous serving counters, a nickel-plated service sink, and lots of under-counter storage for all that was needed to run the kitchen properly. The kitchen's walls are faced with the same white ceramic tile used in the bathrooms. Lit by several utility lights, the kitchen also has considerable natural lighting from windows on the two walls that are out of view. Visible in the far corner, a French door gives light to a small vestibule, and provides access to the basement stairs and entry hall. Placed where a wood-burning stove once was, a gas stove looks entirely at home. It was made over twenty years after the house was completed. Arching purposefully above it is a massive ventilation hood built with a cast-iron frame that was finished with plaster and painted. Out of view to the right, the servants' entrance was through a cheerful glassed-in porch that was also used as their dining room.

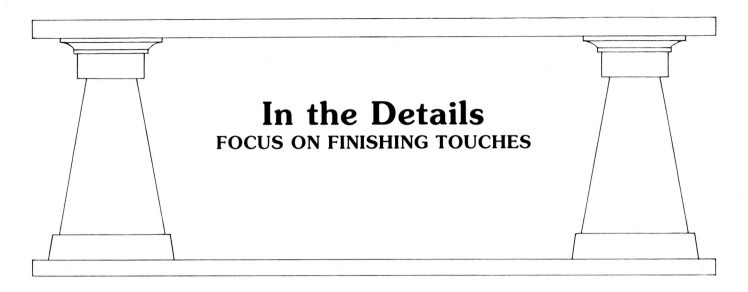

In the Details
FOCUS ON FINISHING TOUCHES

A NOTE ABOUT THE DETAILS

The illustrations that follow are intended as a visual resource of period details, and most of them date from the early twentieth century. Many of the detail illustrations were photographed in houses shown elsewhere in this book. If a detail is an original feature, the date given is the year that the house was built. If it is not exactly known, the approximate date is given. The few illustrations that show newly crafted work are noted as "recent" in their captions. As has been true of other illustrations in this book, the names of contemporary craftspeople whose work appears in an illustration are listed by its figure number in the Credits section.

174. "Aladdin" door knocker, c.1920. The Aladdin Company of Bay City, Michigan, was a well-known manufacturer of "ready-cut" bungalows, which were widely distributed across the United States and Canada. This 6"-high brass knocker, a promotional item, is in the form of their turbaned namesake and logo. To knock, Aladdin's arms and lamp are lifted, thus revealing "Aladdin Homes" engraved underneath.

175. Front door knocker, c.1915, Spokane, Washington. This brass composition of oak leaves and acorns is part of an ensemble of other door hardware with the same motif.

176. Front door knocker, 1914, Oakland, California. This curvaceous and oversized brass knocker is secured by a delicate pin visible at the top, from which it pivots.

177. Combined front door latch and knocker, 1915, Echo Park (Los Angeles), California. This hand-wrought brass design incorporates a knocker above its door latch.

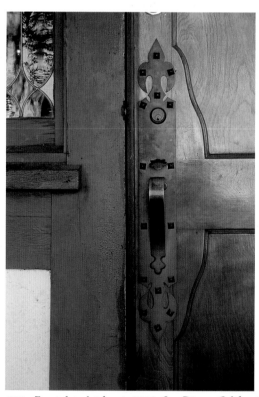

178. Combined front door handle and knocker, 1908, Berkeley, California. In a graceful solution that resembles a giant version of a pull on a built-in cabinet door, the ring of this hand-wrought brass design is grasped and twisted to release the door latch.

179. Front door latch set, 1905, San Diego, California. Secured by square brass rivets, the curves of the fleur-de-lys shapes in the backplate are reflected in the outline of the door's recessed panels. Part of a leaded art-glass window is visible at the left.

180. Front door latch set, c.1915, Echo Park (Los Angeles), California. While appearing to be hand-wrought, this popular design was mass-produced by Pacific Hardware Manufacturing Co. of Los Angeles. Variations of its riveted linear motif were used in similar latch sets and on other matching hardware.

181. Metal push plate for a swinging door in a dining room, 1905, Marin County, California. Wearing through from use, the natural copper finish on this push plate is emerging from beneath an intentionally darkened patina. Twenty-five square rivets secure the plate, and their pattern gives rhythm to a small area.

182. Detail of metalwork on a dining-room sideboard, 1907, Spokane, Washington. Above a serving surface with a mirrored back, two hand-hammered copper strap hinges stretch across a cupboard door. The whimsical repoussé central panel depicts a long-eared elf being tickled by a youthful playmate.

183. Detail of a living-room fireplace with wooden mantel shelf and ceramic-tile facing, 1912, Spokane, Washington. In harmony with the tones of the adjacent wood, each handmade tile of this facing has a reddish mottled glaze framed by deep green. The tiles may have been manufactured by Waco, who produced brick and similar tiles in the state of Washington.

185. Detail of a living-room fireplace with arched ceramic surround and tile facing, 1907, Spokane, Washington. In a house designed by prominent local architect Kirtland Cutter, the flattened "Tudor arch" of this fireplace shows the influence of British Arts and Crafts style that he used in other rooms. This shade of matte-green glaze was popular for both tiles and art pottery. The accent tiles may have been added in the Twenties.

184. Detail of a living-room fireplace with ceramic-tile facing, 1914, Oakland, California. These large, matte-green glazed tiles show the variations that occur during their firing, and which add to their intrinsic beauty. These are similar in color to the green typical of Grueby Pottery.

186. Detail of a living-room fireplace with a ceramic mantel shelf and bracket, tile facing, and accent panel with a peacock (one of a pair), c.1925, Portland, Oregon. This glazed ceramic ensemble, manufactured by Calco Tile of South Gate, California, is characteristic of a type often associated with the better-known Batchelder name. Popular in bungalows of the Twenties, such restrained colors and textured matte glazes lent instant character.

187. Detail of a living-room fireplace, with a ceramic mantel shelf, keystone, tile facing, and accent panel (another part of fireplace in fig. 186), c.1925. The center panel contains a pair of facing peacocks entwined in oak leaves and acorns, and with a squirrel at either side. The chain with a metal tassel operates the chimney's flue mechanism.

188. Detail of a fireplace with brick facing, ceramic mantel shelf, and tile accent panel, 1920s, Echo Park (Los Angeles), California. The color and textural qualities of the brick and ceramic elements are highlighted by a Claycraft tile panel. Within its Spanish Baroque-style frame a view of California mission architecture suggests its roots as a provincial derivative of that style.

189. Detail of a recent wooden living-room fireplace mantel with period ceramic-tile facing, San Diego, California. A contemporary adaptation, this mantel of redwood with lighter birch insets replaced a disfigured original. Its surviving tile facing was salvaged and reset. It resembles Batchelder designs, but was made by California Art Tile of Richmond, California.

190. Detail of wooden living-room fireplace mantel with brick facing and tile accent panel, 1912, Berkeley, California. The painted finish of the low-relief tile landscape panel set into the brick facing suggests that the color was applied after the panel had been fired. The hand-made copper light fixture, one of a pair, is also original.

191. Detail of a living-room fireplace with brick facing and hand-wrought hood, with an adjacent built-in bench, 1912, Albany, Oregon. This is in the D.W. Merrill house, an unusually intact bungalow that is on the National Register of Historic Places.

192. Detail of a brick living-room fireplace (1910) with a recent inscription, Spokane, Washington. Instead of a mantel, a shallow recessed shelf provides display for objects. The first line of the Doxology is painted on the unglazed brick of the shelf.

193. Detail of a recessed living-room fireplace with wooden mantel shelf, brick facing, and decorative brickwork panel, 1916, Seattle, Washington. A panel of Chinese calligraphy, which translates "Where art and books meet," is framed in lighter brick above the mantel.

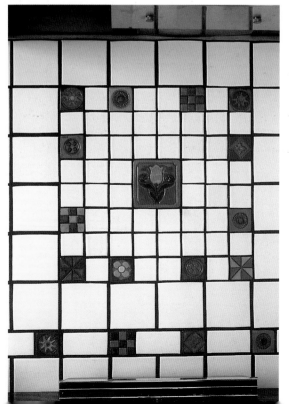

194. Detail of a recent ceramic-tile backsplash in a kitchen, Portland, Oregon. Situated behind the stove, colorful handmade tiles are set into an otherwise plain white tile backsplash.

162

196. Detail of a recent ceramic-tile kitchen backsplash, Spokane, Washington. New green and maroon glazed tiles were chosen to combine with period English accent tiles. A glass switch plate was backpainted to blend in with the tile.

195. Detail showing a kitchen sink cabinet with period tile backsplash and recent ceramic-tile countertop, 1920s, Portland, Oregon. The colors of the original tile backsplash and its small border were closely matched and combined with new white tiles to create the new countertop.

198. Wallpaper-catalog scheme for a dining room, 1914–1915. James Davis imported this lithographed scenic frieze from Germany. It was sold in six different sections (each 42 inches high by 5 feet long) for a total of 35 feet in length. Vignettes depict the monuments of Rome glimpsed between arching trees. The inglenook is not a typical dining room feature.

197. Detail of a ceramic-tile bathroom wall treatment, c.,1925–1930, Los Angeles, California. This vivid orchid wall is trimmed with jade green, and it includes a small border in two shades of the same green and mauve. It is an excellent example of the colored ceramic tiles that became fashionable in the late Twenties and Thirties.

199. Wallpaper-catalog frieze and wainscot treatment for a dining room, 1914–1915. The James Davis catalog presented this 30-inch-high frieze, with its bountiful-fruit motif, as appropriate for use in dining rooms.

200. Detail of a wallpaper frieze in a dining room, 1911, Los Angeles, California. Against lustrous red mahogany woodwork, the rich teal blue background of this frieze highlights its fruit-laden pattern, which was designed and printed to imitate handpainted and stenciled effects.

201. Detail of wallpaper in a dining room, 1904, Portland, Oregon. Part of a scheme that updated a Victorian house, a high wood wainscot with a plate rail was added and doors and casings were replaced. An adaptation of printed fabric patterns of the eighteenth century, the floral wallpaper reflects the Colonial Revival style.

202. Wallpaper-catalog selections of cut-out friezes with matching wall patterns and borders, 1914–1915. James Davis Artistic Paper Hangings imported from Europe these popular "Aerochrome" friezes that were die-cut by precision machinery. Their soft colors were factory-applied by airbrush to highlight the relief of their embossed designs.

203. Detail of a cut-out bedroom wallpaper frieze laid over a striped paper, 1915, La Canada Flintridge, California. Softly colored for use with light-painted woodwork, the swagged floral frieze and the satin-striped wallpaper are in Colonial Revival style. Figures 203–205 are from the Lanterman House, now open to the public as a house museum.

204. Detail of a bedroom wallpaper and a handpainted frieze, 1915. An unknown decorative artist amplified the effect of a typical Colonial Revival-style bedroom paper by artfully extending its meandering design into the frieze area.

205. Detail of bedroom wallpaper with a handpainted and stenciled frieze, 1915. Intended to simulate a woven fabric, the light grays of this leafy design makes it appropriate for use in a bedroom. In the lower frieze area, close to the picture molding, is an oak leaf and acorn border design. Tapestry patterns, in deeper colors, were also popular choices for dining rooms.

206. Detail of upper wall in a den/library, box beams, and stencil treatment, 1911, Seattle, Washington. This detail photograph shows the leather-like textural effect of the background paper in the wall panels, and the metallic colors of the borders and medallions. Art-glass fixtures hang from the box beam intersections.

207. Detail of embossed wallcovering set into living-room wainscot panels, 1907, Spokane, Washington. The texture of this parchment-colored wallcovering, with its overscaled creases and shading, resembles elephant hide. Also original is the hand-wrought copper wall light.

208. Detail of grasscloth wallcovering set into dining-room wainscot panels, 1905, San Diego, California. Part of the original decoration, a simple grasscloth is accented by the dark-stained woodwork. Admired for its texture, grasscloth was widely used in bungalow interiors.

209. Detail of a portière and wallpaper frieze, recent additions to a dining room, 1911, Berkeley, California. The portière of olive linen has been hand-embroidered and appliquéd with a period design adapted from one by Harvey Ellis. The wallpaper frieze of peacocks was reproduced from an English design c.1900 by W. Dennington.

210. Detail of a doorway with a portière in an entry hall, 1905, San Diego, California. Stenciled with a geometric border pattern, this heavy velvet portière survives from the early twentieth century. The slatted screen wall, with useful built-in mirror and hooks, conceals the staircase.

211. Detail of woven fabric frieze in a dining room, 1907, Marin County, California. The colors in this original landscape frieze, a Liberty of London fabric, have faded.

212. Detail of a woven fabric frieze above a music-room wainscot, c.1915, Oakland, California. A landscape frieze of tapestry-like fabric was padded with cotton batting and secured by tacks into narrow wood strips.

214. Stencil schemes for three adjoining rooms, 1917. As seen in this plate from a design-advice book called *Home Interiors,* the use of different color and stencil schemes was recommended in rooms that were open to each other.

213. Detail of a woven fabric frieze above a dining-room wainscot, 1911, Seattle, Washington. This rich tapestry-fabric frieze is of exceptional quality. It was installed in the same way as figure 212.

215. Detail of painted wall finish and stenciled border in a den, 1914, Pasadena, California. The texture and color of the sponged walls blend well with the woodwork.

216. Detail of stenciled borders in a bedroom, 1907, Marin County, California. Stylized leaves and flowers are stenciled in two subtle shades of yellow-green over a cream-color background.

218. Detail of a recent stenciled frieze in a kitchen, San Diego, California. A variation of the Glasgow rose motif is stenciled in repeating pairs as part of a pendant-frieze design.

217. Detail of recently stenciled bedroom frieze, Portland, Oregon. This period stencil design has a gracefully flowing, stylized poppy motif. Popular taste of the Twenties is reflected by the selection of pictures and by the painted bureau that is part of a bedroom set.

219. Detail of a recent handpainted landscape frieze in a breakfast room, Los Angeles, California. In the bright period style of *plein air* paintings, each side of this room reflects seasonal color changes in a rolling, oak-studded California landscape.

220. Detail of handpainted scenic panels in a breakfast room, c.1910, Echo Park (Los Angeles), California. In an unusual original treatment above a wainscot, each of this small room's oil-painted wall panels features a different bird in its leafy bower.

221. Detail of handpainted and stenciled frieze in a dining room, 1907, Spokane, Washington. The saturated colors and boldly twining grapevine motif of the painted frieze is a counterbalance to the heavy woodwork. The spade-shape forms in the leaded art-glass windows suggest a British Arts and Crafts influence.

222. Detail of a copper-leafed and stenciled box-beam ceiling, c.1915, Oakland, California. This striking period treatment has tarnished with age. Overlapped outlines of small copper-leaf sheets are still detectable. Each coffer, framed with double lines, has a flourish of stenciled scrollwork and a shield in each corner.

223. Detail of stenciled box-beam ceiling in an entry hall, 1911, Seattle, Washington. Surrounding the stenciled border of stylized oak leaves and acorns, the excessively contrasting light areas betray their subsequent repainting.

224. Detail of stenciled box-beam ceiling in a dining room, 1911, Seattle, Washington. Within the framing of oak box beams, a softly shaded and stylized grapevine motif was stenciled over each coffer's pale olive background. Single iridescent-glass shaded lights hang from intersecting beams.

225. Five brass lights with painted glass shades hang from a box-beam mounting in a dining room, 1910, Oregon City, Oregon. An unusual original feature, this cruciform box-beam backplate lends importance to the individual lights, which are positioned over a dining-room table.

226. Five beam-mounted copper lights with painted glass shades in a dining room, c.1910, Milwaukee, Oregon. This arrangement of original fixtures is suspended from a structural ceiling beam in a line above the dining-room table. The same arrangement was recommended by Gustav Stickley, in *The Craftsman* magazine of July 1906.

227. Brass fixture base for a single light bulb at intersecting box beams in a living room, 1912, Berkeley, California. In the early twentieth century, bare electric bulbs were sometimes used without any shades, but they would have been of the clear, carbon-filament variety.

228. Wall-mounted copper light fixture with leaded art-glass shade in a stairwell, c.1910, Santa Monica, California. Square rivets secure the bracket to the backplate with its hand-hammered finish and darkened patina. The shade has a simple inverted tulip motif and curved supports.

229. Wall-mounted brass dining-room light fixture with hand-blown art-glass shade, 1911, Seattle, Washington. A hand-hammered finish and an unusual push-button switch is incorporated into the backplate of this fixture. Part of a tapestry-fabric frieze is seen in the background.

230. Wall-mounted copper lantern with an art-glass shade in a stair hall, c.1910, Santa Monica, California. The silhouette of a ship with a billowing sail distinguishes the bracket of this light.

231. Wall-mounted brass light fixture with frosted-glass shade, above a fireplace mantel, 1912, San Francisco, California. The sober visage of a monk embellishes the backplate of this fixture, which is set against a herringbone-patterned brick facing above a mantel.

232. Surface-mounted ceiling fixture with painted metal base and floral decoration on glass shade, c.1920, Portland, Oregon. Ringed with applied floral decoration, this kind of simple fixture was common in bungalow bedrooms, and simpler variations were also standard fare in many of the kitchens.

234. Brass bedroom ceiling fixture with four art-glass lanterns suspended on chains, c.1910, Santa Monica, California. This Craftsman-style fixture would be more likely to be found in a living or dining room, perhaps in combination with matching wall lights.

233. Brass dining-room ceiling fixture suspended on chains and with four frosted-glass shades, c.1910, Echo Park (Los Angeles), California. This popular dining-room fixture style is closely related to the "shower" variety, which placed its bowl-shaped element flush to the ceiling as a backplate for multiple chain-hung lights. Painted wood graining is seen behind it.

235. Copper and art-glass dining-room ceiling fixture by Handel, suspended from a chain, 1912, Spokane, Washington. Original to this room, the fixture has a green patinated finish and umbrella-shaped form. Curved art-glass panels are overlaid with a delicate tracery of willow leaves.

236. Brass and art-glass dining-room ceiling fixture, suspended from a rod and chains, 1910, Spokane, Washington. Converted from a combination gas and electric fixture, finials now indicate where the gas jets were. Glass-beaded fringe shades the glare of concealed electric bulbs.

237. Brass and art-glass den/library ceiling fixture, suspended from chains, and with six leaded art-glass shades, 1911, Seattle, Washington. Building records for this house suggest that Tiffany Studios supplied these fixtures.

238. Three leaded art-glass window panels in a den / library, 1911, Seattle, Washington. The rectilinear designs of these panels derive from the Prairie style and contain a variant of the stylized Glasgow rose.

239. Detail of a living-room inglenook with built-in bench, drawer, and bookcase with leaded-glass doors, c.1915, Spokane, Washington. This area is an expansion of the hearth, and its three-color brick paving provides a contrast in pattern, texture, and height to the adjacent hardwood floor.

240. Built-in pass-through dining-room cabinet, with leaded-glass doors, 1916, Portland, Oregon. This cabinet was provided instead of the usual built-in sideboard. Its use for storing clear glassware also admits light and allows views from the kitchen.

174

241. Built-in dining-room sideboard and adjacent china cabinet with leaded-glass doors, 1906, Los Angeles, California. The room's high ceiling allows extra height for Craftsman-style built-ins. A vintage "area rug" of floral-patterned linoleum survives.

242. Detail of a built-in dining-room sideboard with a pass-through to the kitchen, 1912, Albany, Oregon. Handles on the mirrored panel allow it to slide up for convenient access to and from the kitchen. Also intact are beveled- and leaded-glass cabinet doors and two attached lights. The tapering pilasters of the sideboard echo the column at left. Original flooring of buff-colored hexagonal porcelain tile with a two-color border is an unusual but practical treatment for a dining room.

243. Detail of a built-in dining-room sideboard with a pass-through to the former kitchen, 1910, Oakland, California. When a new kitchen (fig. 90) was added to this house (right background), the old one was converted to a den. This original sideboard with its pass-through opening was left in place. Note the tiny columns with Ionic capitals.

244. Detail of a dining-room sideboard in San Diego, California. Here is an unusually handsome built-in sideboard. In lieu of any art glass, single panes of clear beveled glass are framed in the upper cabinet doors. The slender recessed panels and squares in the lower cabinet are enlivened by green stained-glass insets, and the original brass hardware includes pairs of strap hinges on the cupboard doors. This sideboard is located in the dining room of what has been called the "Pagoda House of North Park" because of its Oriental-inspired exterior detailing. Constructed in 1915, the architect of record is David Owen Dryden.

245. Detail of an inlaid corner and border design of a hardwood floor in a dining room, c.1915, Spokane, Washington. The recently woven area carpet was made to match the floor's design. In this popular period treatment, standard oak flooring was inset with strips of a darker color, which were often a different wood, such as mahogany or walnut.

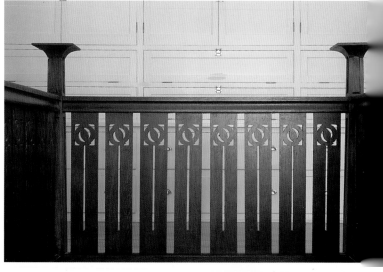

246. Detail of a living-room stair railing with a cut-out design, 1907, Spokane, Washington. The design of this railing closely resembles one illustrated in *The Craftsman* magazine of November 1906. Compare it also to figure 137 in *The Bungalow*.

247. Detail of a stair railing in a second-floor stair hall, 1907, Spokane, Washington. This stylish design strongly recalls British and Scottish Arts and Crafts style. Its cutouts show a variation of the Glasgow rose motif, and its thin newel posts have been lengthened, to terminate in flat, shelf-like caps. A wall of built-in linen storage is visible in the background.

248. Detail of built-in drawers beneath a stair landing, 1911, Santa Monica, California. Definitely in the bungalow planning tradition, this resourceful design has created storage in an unexpected place.

249. Detail of a built-in linen storage cabinet in a hallway, 1914, Berkeley, California. Two bedrooms flank four linen cupboards that have spring-loaded, flip-down doors.

250. Detail of a built-in hallway linen storage cabinet and a door to a stairway, 1914, Santa Cruz, California. Bungalow staircases were often concealed within walls and behind a door. Above three spring-loaded flip-down doors, the cupboard opens to shelving. The other doors open to a kitchen in the corner and a utility closet at the right.

251. Detail of bedroom built-in storage with a wardrobe, drawer, and cupboard unit, 1906, Los Angeles, California. In bungalow bedrooms, such built-ins could reduce the need for bulky furniture.

252. Detail of a built-in bedroom wardrobe, drawer and cupboard storage, sink, and dressing mirror, 1899, Berkeley, California. Made of redwood, this original cabinetry included a discreetly placed sink.

253. Detail of built-in living-room bench and desk, 1923, San Diego, California. This woodwork retains its original grayish stain color.

254. Detail of recent built-in bookcase and cabinet with a hand-painted door panel, San Diego, California. On an inset panel of a cabinet door, artist Michael Wheelden painted a local landscape.

255. Detail of a wooden bedroom door latch (from 1929, in a 1912 house), Berkeley, California. A metal latch, enclosed inside the vertical wooden housing, lifts the crossbar to open the door. This was designed for a rustic, all-wood bedroom that was added in the Twenties.

A NOTE CONCERNING RESOURCES
AND HOW TO LOCATE THEM

There is an ever-increasing range of individual designers, artisans, craftspeople, workshops, manufacturers, antiques dealers, suppliers, and other outlets that are producing or selling furniture, metalwork, ceramics, glass, textiles, wallpapers, and other decorative objects, accessories, and original artwork in the Arts and Crafts style throughout the country. Many excellent resources sell their wares or services nationally by mail order; others prefer to do business on a smaller scale or more local level. In addition, there is a growing number of architects and interior designers who specialize in services for the restoration, renovation, or new construction of Arts and Crafts-style buildings and their interiors.

Many of the photographs in this book show the work of skilled design professionals, fine craftspeople, and other Arts and Crafts-related resources whose work represents a substantial contribution to the revival of interest in the Arts and Crafts Movement. However, this is not intended as a complete or definitive listing. There are many examples of other fine work by contemporary craftspeople that simply did not appear in the rooms that were photographed. Should the work of anyone that does appear in this book remain unidentified, we regret any such unintentional deletions, and wish to apologize to those whose work may remain as yet uncredited. The primary source for our crediting information was provided by the homeowners, and possibly some of that information remained incomplete at the time this book went to press.

There is simply not sufficient space in this book to include a definitive list of every noteworthy resource available today, so instead we have included a listing of related periodicals in lieu of a resource guide. Readers will find that many of the Arts and Craft-related resources that sell their wares nationally may be found as regular advertisers in the majority of the following periodicals. By consulting them routinely for such information, the likelihood of our readers receiving the most current names, addresses, and telephone numbers for such resources is ensured now and in the future. We encourage investigation into each of them. To find various reputable resources that are specific to individual communities may require a bit of sleuthing, and it is usually true that personal recommendations and referrals work best in this regard.

Related Periodicals

American Bungalow
123 South Baldwin Avenue
P.O. Box 756
Sierra Madre, CA 91025-0756
(800) 350-3363

Style: 1900
17 South Main Street
Lambertville, NJ 08530
(609) 397-4104

The Craftsman Homeowner
31 South Grove Street
East Aurora, NY 14052

Old House Interiors
2 Main Street
Gloucester, MA 01930
(800) 462-0211

Old House Journal
2 Main Street

Gloucester, MA 01930
(800) 234-3797

Traditional Building
69-A Seventh Avenue
Brooklyn, NY 11217
(718) 636-0750 (fax)

The Tabby / Arts & Crafts Press
P.O. Box 5217
Berkeley, CA 94705
(510) 849-2117

NOTE: Most of these periodicals also sell related books by mail.

The following is a fine source for books on the Arts and Crafts Movement, and its proceeds also help to support the ongoing maintenance of the Gamble House.
The Gamble House Bookstore
4 Westmoreland Place
Pasadena, CA 91003
(818) 449-4178

(Mail order catalog available by request)

For information regarding the Bungalow Heaven Landmark District and its annual house tour, please contact:
Bungalow Heaven Neighborhood Association
P.O. Box 40672
Pasadena, CA 91114-7672
(818) 585-2172

CREDITS

1. Miscellaneous photo credits

(a) **Figs. 123, 125, 127, 129, 133, 135, 137, 139, 141, 143, 145** were taken by Douglas Keister and used courtesy Bradbury & Bradbury Art Wallpapers (b) **Figs. 93, 94, 122, 124, 126, 128, 132, 134, 136, 138, 140, 142, 144** were taken by Paul Duchscherer and used courtesy Bradbury & Bradbury Art Wallpapers. (c) **Fig. 130** was taken by Frank Cooper. (d) **Fig. 150** was taken by Larry Gable.

2. Archival images

(a) We are especially grateful for the use of the following archival images, which were generously lent courtesy the collection of Timothy Hansen and Dianne Ayres / Arts & Crafts Period Textiles: **Figs. 1, 12, 24, 38, 39, 55, 77, 78, 79, 91, 92, 111, 112.** (b) **Fig. 5:** Courtesy the collection of Erik Kramvik. (c) **Figs. 3, 4, 56, 65, 109:** from the collection of Paul Duchscherer.

Illustration facing page 1: Rug by Blue Hills Studio / Nancy Thomas; fireplace tiles by Tile Restoration Center / Marie Glasse Tapp; pillows by Arts & Crafts Period Textiles / Dianne Ayres; lighting from Collier Lighting / Ron Collier; furniture from Voorhees Craftsman / Mary Ann & Steve Voorhees. **Figs. 2, 26:** Pillow at left by Carol Mead. **Fig. 22:** Front door designed by owner with general contractor Shawn Gabel; lighting by Arroyo Craftsman; architect: Doug Ewing. **Fig. 28:** Tile by McIntyre Tile Company, Inc.; fireplace hood by Walter Morc Company, Inc. **Fig. 29:** Sofa fabric by Clarence House; rugs from Essa Mokri; lighting by Nowell's. **Fig. 30:** Copper smoke guard designed by Rob Winovich and made by Scott Blair. **Fig. 31:** Pillow at left by Carol Mead; pillow at right from Brian Coleman. **Fig. 18:** Renovation architect: Hoshide Williams / Robert I. Hoshide, principal architect; project architect: Grace Schlitt. **Figs. 42, 45** (at left): Pillows by Arts & Crafts Period Textiles / Dianne Ayres. **Fig. 43:** Lampshade (at right) by Sue Johnson. **Fig. 46:** Floorlamp by Aurora Studios / Michael Adams. **Fig. 47:** Curtains by Arts & Crafts Period Textiles / Dianne Ayres. **Fig. 53:** Restoration by Elder Vides; furniture by L. & J.G. Stickley, Inc.; floorlamp by Quiet Time, Inc. / Louis Glesman. **Fig. 58:** Ceiling light by Arroyo Craftsman. **Fig. 60:** Table lamp by Rejuvenation Lamp & Fixture Company. **Fig. 61:** Restoration Architect: Martin Eli Weil; interior designer / consultant: Roger L. Conant Williams. **Fig. 67:** Frieze stenciled by Pinson & Ware; curtains and table linens by Arts & Crafts Period Textiles / Dianne Ayres. **Fig. 68:** Pillows by Arts & Crafts Period Textiles / Dianne Ayres. **Fig. 69.** Rug by Blue Hills Studio / Nancy Thomas; curtains and table linens by Arts & Crafts Period Textiles / Dianne Ayres. **Fig. 70:** Furniture by L & J.G. Stickley, Inc. **Fig. 71:** Lampshade (at left) by Sue Johnson. **Fig. 72:** Renovation: The Johnson Partnership / Larry and Lani Johnson. **Fig. 73:** Furniture by L. & J.G. Stickley, Inc.; restoration consultant: Jim Gibson; lighting from Gibson & Gibson; art glass by Heather Trimlett; woodwork by Walt Diebold. **74:** Interior design by Four Dimensions / Catherine Phelps. **Fig. 75:** Wallpaper by Bradbury & Bradbury Art Wallpapers. **Fig. 81:** Restoration consultant: John Benriter. **Fig. 84:** Interior design by Don Shelman / Avenue Antiques. **Fig. 85:** Architect: Joseph W. Greif; cooktop by Gaggenau; dishwasher by Asko; hardware from Old & Elegant. **Fig. 86:** Refrigerator by Sub-Zero; oven by Gaggenau. **Fig. 87:** General contractor: Marshall White Construction; cabinetwork by Marnell Cabinetry / Mike Marnell; lighting from Collier Lighting / Ron Collier; Roman shades and table linens by Arts & Crafts Period Textiles / Dianne Ayres; backsplash tile (background) by Tile Restoration Center / Marie Glasse Tapp; copper hood by Lowell Chaput; hardware by Buffalo Studios / Tony Smith; stove by Viking; china (on counter) by Roycroft Shops, Inc. **Fig. 88:** General contractor: Shawn Gabel; interior designers: Colleen Monahan and owner; refrigerator by Sub-Zero; cooktop and oven by Dacor; lighting by Arroyo Craftsman; hardware by Craftsman Hardware / Chris Efker. **Fig. 89:** Light boxes by Nowell's; tile by Heath Ceramics; stove by U.S. Range. **Fig. 90:** Architect: Jarvis Architects / Glen Jarvis; ceiling light by Arroyo Craftsman; cooktop by Russell Range; sink fittings by Chicago Faucet. **Fig. 98:** Restoration architect: Martin Eli Weil; interior designer / consultant: Roger L. Conant Williams. **Fig. 99:** Bed by James Ipekjian; nightstand (at left) by L. & J.G. Stuckley, Inc.; curtains by Arts & Crafts Period Textiles / Dianne Ayres. **Fig. 101:** Bed by Debey Zito Fine Furniture / Debey Zito, with handcarved bats on headboard by Terry Schmitt; copper table lamp (at right) by Arnold Benetti; lampshade (only) on table lamp (at left) by Sue Johnson; pair of wall lights by Steph Zlott; floor-lamp (at left) by Barclay Moore; wallpaper by Bradbury & Bradbury Art Wallpapers; painting (over bureau) by Olaf Palm. **Fig. 102:** Frieze painted by Brushworks / Karen Weiner; rug from Floordesigns; Roman shade fabric by Arthur Sanderson and Sons; lighting from Collier Lighting / Ron Collier; bed linens by Anichini Bedding. **Fig. 103:** General contractor: Marshall White Construction; bed, nightstands, and built-ins by Marnell Cabinetry / Mike Marnell; hardware by Buffalo Studios / Tony Smith; rug by Blue Hills Studio / Nancy Thomas; Roman shades by Arts & Crafts Period Textiles / Dianne Ayres. **Fig. 105:** Construction and cabinetry by John Wick and Bud Gilson. **Fig. 113:** Restoration by Elder Vides. **Fig. 114:** Sink and toilet from Sunrise Salvage; light from Omega Salvage. **Fig. 117:** Tile from Pratt and Larson; lighting by Rejuvenation Lamp & Fixture Company. **Fig. 118:** Wallpaper by Arthur Sanderson and Sons; tile and slate flooring by Pratt and Larson; sink and toilet by Crane; lighting from Rejuvenation Lamp & Fixture Company; glass shelf by Gatco; towel bars by Franklin Brass. **Fig. 119:** Interior designer: John Zanakis / House of Orange; design consultant and finish carpentry: Timothy Hansen; tile (at wainscot) from Heath Ceramics; tub from American Standard; sink top (salvaged) from The Sink Factory; towel bars from Sunrise Salvage; hardware by Chicago Renaissance; recessed lighting / fan grilles from Reggio Register; lighting (at left / to match existing) made by John Zanakis / House of Orange. **Fig. 120:** General contractor: Marshall White Construction; cabinetry by Marnell Cabinetry / Mike Marnell; hardware by Buffalo Studios / Tony Smith; lighting from Collier Lighting / Ron Collier; rug by Blue Hills Studio / Nancy Thomas; tile mural painted by Brenda Rose. **Fig. 121:** General contractor: Marshall White Construction; cabinetry by Marnell Cabinetry / Mike Marnell; hardware by Buffalo Studios / Tony Smith; lighting from Collier Lighting / Ron Collier; tile (floor and wall field) by Architerra Northwest; tile (borders) by Dale Marsh / Tile Artisans. **Figs. 123,** **125, 127, 129, 133, 135, 137, 139, 141, 143, 145:** Wallpaper by Bradbury & Bradbury Art Wallpapers / Bruce Bradbury; wallpaper artwork by Scott Cazet; wallpaper design layout by Bradbury & Bradbury's Design Service / Therese Tierney, with Diana Woodbridge; design consultant / room stylist: Paul Duchscherer; pillows, curtains and most other textiles by Arts & Crafts Period Textiles / Dianne Ayres. The Craftsman Home / Lee Jester generously lent additional furnishings, accessories and artwork, as required, for these photographs (except for figs. 123, 125, 141, 143). Additional individual credits for these photographs: **Figs. 123, 125:** Paperhanging by Michael Keith. **Figs. 127, 129, 133, 135, 137, 145:** Paperhanging by Peter Bridgman. **Fig. 139:** Paperhanging by Heidi Risse. **Fig. 141, 143:** Paperhanging by Helen Boutell. **Fig. 127:** Settle and painting (at right) lent courtesy of Therese Tierney. **Fig. 135:** Framed print (at center) by Kathleen West; flanking prints by Anita Munman. **Fig. 137:** Mirror on mantel by Holton Furniture & Frame / Timothy Holton; pillow (at right) by Carol Mead; framed print by Anita Munman; two (taller) green ceramic vases by Roycroft Potters / Janice McDuffie; fireplace fender and candlesticks lent courtesy of Therese Tierney. **Fig. 139:** Framed print by Kathleen West; table lamp by Bob Pappas; ceiling light fixture by Sue Johnson. **Fig. 141:** Copper and mica lamp (in far left corner) by Audel Davis. **Fig. 147:** Interior design by Paul Duchscherer; bed and night table by Debey Zito Fine Furniture / Debey Zito; portière by Arts & Crafts Period Textiles / Dianne Ayres; Japanese shoji screens and cabinet (below) from Nakura, Inc.; light from Soko Hardware; painting (above bed) by John Freed; finish carpentry by Terry Schmidt. **Fig. 149:** Wall paintings cleaned and restored by Pinson & Ware / Ed Pinson and Debra Ware; restoration consultant: John Benriter. **Fig. 151:** General contractor: Dean Poppe; tub from Omega Salvage; fixture hardware by Sign of the Crab; sink and toilet by St. Thomas; lighting by Rejuvenation Lamp & Fixture Company. **Fig. 189:** Restoration consultant: Jim Gibson; finish carpentry by Walt Diebold. **Fig. 194:** Tiles from Pratt and Larson. **Fig. 195:** Countertop tiles from Pratt and Larson; sink hardware by Chicago Faucet; linoleum flooring by Farbo. **Fig. 205:** Painted frieze restored by Pinson and Ware. **Fig. 209:** Portière by Arts & Crafts Period Textiles / Dianne Ayres; frieze by Bradbury & Bradbury Art Wallpapers. **Fig. 217:** Stencil design from Helen Foster Stencils; stenciling by Craig Kuhns. **Fig. 218:** Stenciling by Don and Karen Covington. **Fig. 219:** Frieze painted by Ed Pinson of Pinson and Ware. **Fig. 234:** Stencil design from Helen Foster Stencils; stenciling by Zvia Weinstein. **Fig. 241:** Renovation architect: Tracy A. Stone; painted finishes by Span Parks. **Fig. 243:** Renovation architect: Jarvis Architects / Glen Jarvis.

BIBLIOGRAPHY

Anderson, Timothy J.; Moore, Eudora M.; Winter, Robert W. (eds.). *California Design 1910*. Pasadena, Calif.; California Design Publications, 1974. Reprint, Santa Barbara, Calif.: and Salt Lake City, Utah: Peregrine Smith, Inc., 1980.

Bernhardi, Robert. *The Buildings of Berkeley*. Oakland, Calif.: Berkeley Architectural Heritage Association and Forest Hills Press, 1971.

Bosley, Edward R.; Clark, Robert Judson; Makinson, Randell L. *Last of the Ultimate Bungalows: The William R. Thorsen House of Greene and Greene*. Pasadena, Calif.: The Gamble House, USC, 1996 (exhibition catalog).

Bowman, Leslie Greene. *American Arts and Crafts: Virtue in Design*. Los Angeles, Calif.: Los Angeles County Museum of Art, 1990.

Brooks, H. Allen. *Frank Lloyd Wright and the Prairie School*. New York: George Braziller, Inc., in association with Cooper-Hewitt Museum, 1984.

Brown, Henry Collins. *Book of Home Building and Decoration*. New York: Doubleday, Page & Company, 1912.

Callen, Althea. *Angels in the Studio: Women Artists of the Arts and Crafts Movement 1870-1914*. London: The Architectural Press, 1979. Reprint (as *Women Artists of the Arts and Crafts Movement 1870-1914*). New York: Pantheon Books, 1979.

Cerny, Susan Dinkelspiel. *Berkeley Landmarks*. Berkeley, Calif.: Berkeley Architectural Heritage Association, 1994.

Clark, Robert Judson (ed.). *The Arts and Crafts Movement in America 1876–1916*. Princeton, N.J.: Princeton University Press, 1972.

Comstock, William Phillips. *Bungalows, Camps and Mountain Houses*. New York: W.T. Comstock Company, 1915 (revised from original edition of 1908). Reprint, Washington, D.C.: The American Institute of Architects Press, 1990.

Cooper, Jeremy. *Victorian and Edwardian Decor*. New York: Abbeville Press, 1987.

Current, William R., and Current, Karen. *Greene & Greene: Architects in the Residential Style*. Fort Worth, Texas: Amon Carter Museum of Western Art, 1974.

Dillaway, Theodore M. *Decoration of the School and Home*. Springfield, Mass.: Milton Bradley Company, 1914.

Fleming, John, and Pevsner, Nikolaus. *The Penguin Dictionary of Architecture*. Harmondsworth, Middlesex, England: Penguin Books Ltd., 1979.

Freudenheim, Leslie Mandelson, and Sussman, Elisabeth. *Building with Nature: Roots of the San Francisco Bay Region Tradition*. Santa Barbara, Calif., and Salt Lake City, Utah: Peregrine Smith, Inc., 1974.

Frohne, Henry W. (ed.). *Home Interiors*. Grand Rapids, Mich.: *Good Furniture Magazine*, 1917.

Gebhard, David, and Winter, Robert. *Los Angeles: An Architectural Guide*. Layton, Utah: Gibbs Smith / Peregrine Smith Books, 1994.

Gebhard, David; Sandweiss, Eric; Winter, Robert. *The Guide to Architecture in San Francisco and Northern California*. Layton, Utah: Gibbs Smith / Peregrine Smith Books, 1985.

Gere, Charlotte, and Whiteway, Michael. *Nineteenth Century Design: From Pugin to Mackintosh*. London: George Weidenfield and Nicolson Ltd., 1993. Reprint, New York: Harry N. Abrams, Inc., 1994.

Gordon-Van Tine Company. *117 House Designs of the Twenties*. Davenport, Iowa: Gordon-Van Tine Company, 1923. Reprint,

Mineola, N.Y.: The Atheneum of Philadelphia and Dover Publications, Inc., 1992.

Goss, Peter L., and Trapp, Kenneth R. *The Bungalow Lifestyle and the Arts & Crafts Movement in the Intermountain West*. Salt Lake City, Utah: Utah Museum of Fine Arts, University of Utah, 1995 (exhibition catalog).

Jones, Robert T. (ed.). *Authentic Small Houses of the Twenties*. New York: Harper and Brothers Publishers, 1929. Reprint, New York: Dover Publications, Inc., 1987.

Kaplan, Wendy. *"The Art That Is Life": The Arts and Crafts Movement in America, 1875-1920*. Boston, Mass.: Little, Brown and Company, 1987.

Keeler, Charles Augustus. *The Simple Home*. San Francisco, Calif.: P. Elder, 1904. Reprint, Santa Barbara, Calif., and Salt Lake City, Utah: Peregrine Smith, Inc., 1979.

King, Anthony D. *The Bungalow: The Production of a Global Culture*. London: Routledge & Kegan Paul, 1984. Reprint, New York: Oxford University Press, 1995.

Lancaster, Clay. *The American Bungalow*. New York: Abbeville Press, 1985.

Loizeaux, J.D. *Classic Houses of the Twenties*. Elizabeth, N.J.: J.D. Loizeaux Lumber Company and the Loizeaux Builders Supply Co., 1927. Reprint, Mineola, N.Y.: The Atheneum of Philadelphia and Dover Publications, Inc., 1992.

Makinson, Randell L. *Greene and Greene: Architecture as Fine Art*, Salt Lake City, Utah: Gibbs M. Smith, Inc. / Peregrine Smith Books, 1977.

———. *Greene and Greene: Furniture and Related Designs*. Salt Lake City, Utah: Gibbs M. Smith, Inc. / Peregrine Smith Books, 1979.

Morgan Woodworking Organization. *Building With Assurance*. Oshkosh, Wis.: Morgan Woodworking Organization, 1921.

Naylor, Gillian. *The Arts and Crafts Movement*. London: Studio Vista, 1971.

Parry, Linda (ed.). *William Morris*. London: Philip Wilson Publishers Ltd., 1996. Reprint, New York: Harry N. Abrams, Inc., 1996.

Peisch, Mark L. *The Chicago School of Architecture*. New York: Random House, 1964.

Pool, Mary Jane; Seebohm, Caroline (eds.). *House and Garden. 20th Century Decorating, Architecture, and Gardens*. New York: Holt, Rinehart and Winston, 1980.

Saylor, Henry H. *Bungalows*. New York: Robert M. McBride and Co., 1911.

Sears, Roebuck and Company. *Sears, Roebuck Catalog of Houses, 1926*. Chicago, Ill., and Philadelphia, Pa.: Sears, Roebuck and Company, 1926. Reprint, New York: The Atheneum of Philadelphia and Dover Publications, Inc., 1991.

Sherwin-Williams Company Decorative Department. *Your Home and Its Decoration* (n.p.): The Sherwin-Williams Company, 1910.

Smith, Bruce, and Yamamoto, Yoshiko. *The Beautiful Necessity: Decorating With Arts and Crafts*. Layton, Utah: Gibbs Smith, Publisher, 1996.

Stickley, Gustav. *The Best of Craftsman Homes*. Santa Barbara, Calif., and Salt Lake City, Utah: Peregrine Smith, Inc., 1979. (Includes plans from Stickley's *Craftsman Homes* (1909) and *More Craftsman Homes* (1912).

———. *Craftsman Bungalows: 59 Homes from "The Craftsman."* Mineola, N.Y.: Dover Publications, Inc., 1988. (This book reprints thirty-six articles selected from issues of *The Craftsman* magazine published between December 1903 and August 1916.)

Trapp, Kenneth R. (ed.). *The Arts and Crafts Movement in California: Living the Good Life*. New York: Abbeville Press Publishers, 1993.

Vanderwalker, F.N. *New Stencils and Their Use*. Chicago: Frederick J. Drake & Co., 1918.

Via, Maria, and Searle, Marjorie (eds.). *Head, Heart and Hand: Elbert Hubbard and the Roycrofters*. Rochester, N.Y.: University of Rochester Press, 1994.

Von Holst, Hermann Valentin. *Country and Suburban Homes of the Prairie Period*. (Originally published: *Modern American Homes*. Chicago: American Technical Society, 1913, c.1912.) Reprint, New York: Dover Publications, Inc., 1982.

Watkinson, Ray. *William Morris as Designer*. London: Cassell Ltd., 1967.

Wilson, Henry L. *California Bungalows of the Twenties*. Los Angeles, Calif.: Henry L. Wilson (n.d.). Reprint, Mineola, N.Y.: Dover Publications, Inc., 1993.

Winter, Robert (text), and Vertikoff, Alexander (photographs). *American Bungalow Style*. New York: Simon & Schuster, 1996.

Winter, Robert. *The California Bungalow*. Los Angeles, Calif.: Hennessey & Ingalls, Inc., 1980.

Woodbridge, Sally, and Montgomery, Roger. *A Guide to Architecture in Washington State*. Seattle, Wash.; University of Washington Press, 1980.

Woodbridge, Sally (ed.). *Bay Area Houses: New Edition*. Layton, Utah: Gibbs M. Smith, Inc., 1988.

Wright, Agnes Foster. *Floors, Furniture and Color*. Lancaster, Pa.: Armstrong Cork Company, Linoleum Division, 1924.